Muslim-Christian Relations

FAITH MEETS FAITH

An Orbis Series in Interreligious Dialogue
Paul F. Knitter, General Editor
Editorial Advisors
John Berthrong
Julia Ching
Diana Eck
Karl-Josef Kuschel
Lamin Sanneh
George E. Tinker
Felix Wilfred

In the contemporary world, the many religions and spiritualities stand in need of greater communication and cooperation. More than ever before, they must speak to, learn from, and work with each other in order both to maintain their vital identities and to contribute to fashioning a better world.

FAITH MEETS FAITH seeks to promote interreligious dialogue by providing an open forum for exchanges among followers of different religious paths. While the Series wants to encourage creative and bold responses to questions arising from contemporary appreciations of religious plurality, it also recognizes the multiplicity of basic perspectives concerning the methods and content of interreligious dialogue.

Although rooted in a Christian theological perspective, the Series does not endorse any single school of thought or approach. By making available to both the scholarly community and the general public works that represent a variety of religious and methodological viewpoints, FAITH MEETS FAITH seeks to foster an encounter among followers of the religions of the world on matters of common concern.

FAITH MEETS FAITH SERIES

Muslim-Christian Relations

Past, Present, Future

Ovey N. Mohammed, S.J.

ORBIS BOOKS

Maryknoll, New York 10545

The Catholic Foreign Mission Society of America (Maryknoll) recruits and trains people for overseas missionary service. Through Orbis Books, Maryknoll aims to foster the international dialogue that is essential to mission. The books published, however, reflect the opinions of their authors and are not meant to represent the official position of the society.

Selections from *Al Qu'r'an: A Contemporary Translation*, translator Ahmed Ali, copyright © 1988, reproduced by courtesy of Princeton University Press.
Map of the expansion of the Islamic empire in the early years, adapted from Albert Hourani, *A History of the Arab Peoples*, copyright © 1991, courtesy of The Belknap Press of Harvard University.
Map of the Islamic world adapted from Byron L. Haines and Frank L. Cooley, editors, *Christians and Muslims Together,* copyright © 1987, courtesy of The Geneva Press, Louisville, Kentucky.
Scripture quotations are taken from the New Revised Standard Version, *The New Oxford Annotated Bible with the Apocrypha*, copyright © 1991, 1994 by the Division of Christian Education of the National Council of Churches, published by Oxford University Press, Inc.

Library of Congress Cataloging in Publication Data

#401353 19
Mohammed, Ovey N. (Ovey Nelson), 1933-
    Muslim-Christian relations : past, present, future / Ovey N. Mohammed
        p. cm. — (Faith meets faith series)
    Includes index.
    ISBN 1-57075-257-5 (pbk.)
    1. Islam—Relations—Christianity. 2. Christianity and other religions—Islam I. Title II. Series: Faith meets faith.
BP172.M59   1999
261.2'7—dc21   98-47530
                                                              CIP

Contents

Maps

Introduction

Nowhere is the agenda for the interreligious dialogue more pressing than with the adherents of the two largest religious communities, Christians and Muslims, because together these two communities encompass nearly half of the world's population. Though both communities are growing rapidly, Islam is the faster growing of the two religions. Islam is not confined to the Middle East. Like Christianity, it has an international membership. The majority of Muslims live in South and West Asia and West and East Africa. Indonesia has the largest Muslim population, about one hundred and fifty million. India's Muslim community, although a minority, numbers one hundred and twenty million, a population that is larger than that of the Arab Muslim population of the Middle East. Pakistan and Bangladesh follow with roughly one hundred and ninety-two million members each. In Africa north of the Sahara the Muslim population is about one hundred million. South of the Sahara it is around one hundred and thirty million. In sixty countries Muslims comprise the majority. In another fifteen nations they comprise a substantial minority. In Europe, Islam is already the second largest religious tradition, collectively and in virtually every country. Demographers predict that in the early years of the next century, Muslims will surpass Jews as the second largest community in the United States and Canada. Today, only 15 percent of the Muslim world lives in the Middle East.[1]

These are the dimensions of the worldwide Muslim-Christian dialogue. Hence, even from a pragmatic point of view, the pressing issues facing our increasingly interdependent world should stimulate all Christians and Muslims to review and reconsider their relations with each other.

This book is an attempt at such a review. It will reflect on obstacles and opportunities facing contemporary Christian-Muslim relations. There are obstacles because most Christians have very little understanding of the faith of Muslims in spite of the long history of association between the two communities. To help them prepare for dialogue with Muslims, chapter 1 is a concise introduction to Islam for Christians. It will center on Muhammad the man, his message as recorded in the Qur'an, and his community. It will explain the place of law in the Islamic understanding of revelation and its role in unifying the Muslim community, how the community came to be divided into Sunnis and Shi'ites, and how they differ from one another. Because spirituality is a rich area for dialogue, the introduction will examine the Sufi path to God and compare it with spiritual practices found in the Bible and the Christian tradition, including *The Spiritual Exercises* of St. Ignatius of Loyola.

There are obstacles, too, because the story of past relations between Christians and Muslims is not a happy one, for reasons that are cultural, political, and economic as well as religious. Because these obstacles are still present in the current dialogue, our reflection will try to highlight some of them. Chapter 2 focuses on the cultural, political, and economic obstacles. More concretely, it examines the Christian response to religious and cultural diversity before the birth of Islam; the Muslim response to the same issues after the birth of Islam, the Western Christian encounter with Islam through the crusades, and the impact that Islamic scholarship had on the development of Western thought; the status of Christians living under Arab and Ottoman rule; the Western domination of the Muslim world through colonialism, and the role that Christian missionaries played in undermining the Islamic faith; and the reasons for the collapse of the Ottoman Empire after World War I and for the resurgence of Islam after World War II. The chapter concludes with a look at the issue of human rights in Christianity and in Islam as the adherents of both religions struggle together to face the future on the eve of the third millennium of the common era.

Chapter 3 examines the theological obstacles in the encounter. It explores the reasons for the Christian rejection of Islam right up to the twentieth century. It then tries to explain why Catholics, after the collapse of colonialism, took the opportunity to develop a positive theology of Islam that not only accepts Islam as part of God's plan of salvation but also leaves Catholics free to accept the prophethood of Muhammad after Jesus and the Qur'an as revelation after the gospels. The chapter attempts to show that this positive attitude to Islam is based on the new Catholic understanding of revelation and the role of the Holy Spirit in salvation. It also investigates whether or not the new understanding of revelation can be harmonized with the Qur'anic view and tries to explain why Abraham, our common forefather in faith, can play a decisive role in bringing the followers of the two largest religious communities closer together.

Chapter 4 considers the prospects for Muslim-Christian collaboration by reflecting on how Christian and Muslim perspectives on salvation, mission, and dialogue can negatively or positively affect these prospects. It will do so by examining the Muslim perspective on these issues, the Protestant response to the Muslim position, how the Roman Catholic response differs from the Protestant, and how this difference is hindering Protestant efforts and helping Catholic efforts to move the Muslim-Christian relationship forward. The chapter concludes with a focus on the Muslim-Christian encounter in North America and Britain.

As for the book itself, I have tried to present the material in a way that is intelligible to the general reader. Persons interested in a more comprehensive treatment of the issues can consult the notes and bibliography. In the event that the book is used by study groups, there are questions for discussion as well as suggestions for further reading at the end of each chapter. At the end of the book there is a glossary of Islamic terms used in the text and a list of useful addresses of periodicals and organizations devoted to Muslim-Christian dialogue.

Being a Canadian Jesuit, I wrote with a North American and British Christian readership in mind. In the spirit of dialogue, however, I hope that what I have written is also of interest to Muslims. Finally, I should like to thank William R. Burrows, managing editor of Orbis Books, for inviting me to write the book, and for his encouragement and invaluable suggestions in the writing of it.

1

Islam

An Introduction for Christians

MUHAMMAD

In Muslim countries at dawn each morning a crier calls the faithful to prayer by proclaiming:

> God is most great!
> God is most great!
> I testify that there is no god but God.
> I testify that Muhammad is the prophet of God.
> Arise and pray; arise and pray.

Who is this Muhammad to whom the crier refers?

Muhammad was born into a well-established but impoverished family in Mecca in 570. His early life was cradled in tragedy, for his father 'Abd Allah died a few days before he was born, his mother Amina when he was six, and his grandfather 'Abd al-Muttalib, who cared for him after his mother's death, when he was eight. He was then adopted by his uncle, Abu Talib, and spent his boyhood roaming the hills around Mecca tending his uncle's flocks. Thus from an early age he grew accustomed to the loneliness of being an orphan and the desolation of the Arabian desert.

The Arabia into which Muhammad was born was essentially a tribal and polytheistic society. The city of Mecca, which lay along the trade routes between the Yemen and the Levant, was a commercial center. As well as being a place for trade, it had the greater asset of being a place of pilgrimage for the many gods of the peninsula.

Given the fact that Mecca was a commercial center, Muhammad took up the caravan business upon reaching maturity. In 590, at the age of twenty, he entered the service of a rich widow named Khadija. Though she was fifteen years his senior, she proposed marriage to him when he was twenty-five. He accepted and during her lifetime took no other partner. Their married life was a happy one. Khadija bore him two sons and four daughters. The sons died in infancy.

Though married, Muhammad loved solitude and often retired to a cave on Mount Hira, in the hills he had roamed as a boy. There he reflected on the cruel strife of his compatriots, the endless quarrels among the tribes visiting the Meccan shrines, and the general immorality of his day.

Through vigils and meditation, often lasting through the night, Allah's reality became for him increasingly evident and awesome. Allah was not one God among many, as many of Muhammad's compatriots believed, nor even the greatest of gods. Allah was the one and only God. Soon from the mountain cave on Mount Hira was to sound the greatest phrase of the Arabic language: *La ilāha illā' Llāh!* There is no god but God!

But first Muhammad had to receive his commission from God, as did Abraham, Moses, Samuel, Isaiah, and others before him. One night, around 610, when Muhammad was alone in his cave, the angel Gabriel appeared to him in the form of a man. Gabriel said to him, "Recite!" The frightened Muhammad replied, "I am not a reciter." Gabriel, not taking no for an answer, physically overpowered him and then released him. The same exchange took place. Again Muhammad said, "I am not a reciter." Again Gabriel overpowered him. Finally, after Gabriel's third command to "Recite!" Muhammad said, "What shall I recite?" And Gabriel revealed the first passage of the "Recitation":

Recite: In the Name of thy Lord who created, created man of a blood-clot. Recite: And thy Lord is the Most Generous, who by the Pen taught Man what he did not know (Q 96:1-3).

The night on which Muhammad received his call is known as the Night of Power. According to the Qur'an, it "is better than a thousand months; in it the angels and the Spirit descend, by the leave of their Lord, upon every command. Peace it is, till the rising of dawn" (Q 97:3-5).

Recovering from the experience, Muhammad hurried home full of doubts and misgivings. Was he receiving a revelation from God, or was he going mad? He went through what Western mystics have called "the dark night of the soul." For twenty-two years the recitations came again and again, in the form of a voice and a vision, and the command was always the same—to recite: "O thou in thy mantle, arise, and warn! Thy Lord magnify, thy robes purify and defilement flee!" (Q 74:1-5). Mantles, since the time of Elijah, have been a symbol of prophetic authority. Moreover, Muhammad's auditions and visions, his doubts, and his reluctance to accept the divine mandate are reminiscent of the call of many Old Testament prophets such as Isaiah, Jeremiah, and Ezekiel.

For the most part the people of Mecca responded to Muhammad's message with hostility. Many factors contributed to this reaction, but perhaps the main one was that its uncompromising monotheism threatened not only polytheistic beliefs but also the considerable revenue that was coming to Mecca from pilgrimages. One is reminded of the first preaching of Christianity at Ephesus, where the silversmiths complained that

> Paul has persuaded and drawn away a considerable number of people by saying that gods made with hands are not gods. And there is danger not only that this trade of ours may come into disrepute but also that the temple of the great goddess Artemis will be scorned, and she will be deprived of her majesty that brought all Asia and the world to worship her (Acts 19:26-27).

Muhammad and his converts were heckled, ridiculed, and even subjected to persecution. The situation worsened after Muhammad, in 619, lost both his wife Khadija and his uncle, Abu Talib, who were his faithful supporters.

When all appeared to be lost, new possibilities arose in 621: some inhabitants from Yathrib, a city north of Mecca, on hearing Muhammad's message, invited him and his followers to immigrate to their city. The invitation was accepted as a vindication from God. After receiving their pledge that they would worship Allah as the one and only God, Muhammad and his followers secretly migrated to Yathrib in June 622.

Muslims regard the migration *(hijra)* as the turning point of world history and date their calendar from this year. Yathrib soon became known as Medinat al-Nabi, the City of the Prophet, and then by contraction, as Medina. In Medina, when the religious vision of the Meccan revelations had to be put into communal practice, the despised preacher had to become a masterful politician and statesman.

For the remaining ten years of his life, Muhammad's personal history merged with that of the Medinese commonwealth, of which he became head. Most important, he had to settle the struggle with the Meccans for the mind of Arabia. Battles were fought. In Badr, in 624, a small group of Medinese won a victory over a Meccan army many times larger. The following year witnessed a reversal: the Meccans gained a slim victory near Uhud. The Meccans followed up this victory in 627 by laying siege to Medina to force the Muslims to capitulate. They failed. In 630, eight years after Muhammad's migration to Medina from Mecca, he who left as a fugitive returned as a conqueror. Muhammad did not press his victory. In his hour of triumph he forgave his persecutors. Making his way to the Ka'ba, a temple Muslims claim was built by Abraham and his son Ishmael, he rededicated it to Allah, the one and only God.

That Muhammad's call led him to be not only a religious but also a military and political leader points to the scope of his perceived prophetic task, as was the case with many prophets in the Old Testament. For example, Samuel was a man of action, at once a prophet and a military leader

(1 Sm 15). In David's court, the prophet Nathan exercised a very powerful influence in the affairs of Israel (2 Sm 7:1-17; 2 Sm 12:1f.). And Moses took up arms against idolaters (Ex 32:27-29), as did Elijah (1 Kgs 18:40).

For Muslims, Muhammad spoke and acted on God's behalf; that is, he was a prophet. He was human, and there was no trace of divinity in him. However, he was no ordinary mortal. For Muslims he is blessed among men, just as for Christians Mary is blessed among women. And, indeed, "the role of Muhammad in Islam is in some ways analogous to that of the Virgin Mary in Christianity. The annunciation to Mary, like the revelation to Muhammad, came through the angel Gabriel. Mary, a virgin, produced a Son, while Muhammad, 'unlettered' *(ummi)*, produced a Book. Muhammad's 'illiteracy,' like Mary's virginity, is of profound metaphysical and spiritual significance."[1]

THE QUR'AN

The Qur'an is the record of the revelations received by Muhammad between his call in 610 and his death in 632. These revelations were collected and edited within a period of some twenty-five years into more or less the form in which they are found today.

Four-fifths the length of the New Testament, the Qur'an is divided into one hundred and fourteen chapters, or *suras*, each containing verses called *ayat*, or "signs" of God. Generally speaking, the longer chapters were revealed in Medina and the shorter in Mecca. Thus the arrangement of the chapters as it exists today is not the order in which the revelations were received. When the sacred texts were put together in the days of the caliph Uthman (644-56), they were arranged in order of decreasing length. An exception to this is the brief prayer that forms chapter 1 of the Qur'an. The prayer is known as the *Fatiha* and corresponds in use to the Lord's Prayer in Christianity. It reads as follows:

In the Name of God, the Merciful, the Compassionate. Praise belongs to God, the Lord of all Being, the All-merciful, the All-compassionate, the Master of the Day of Doom. Thee only we serve; to Thee alone we pray for succour. Guide us in the straight path, the path of those whom Thou hast blessed, not of those against whom thou art wrathful, nor of those who are astray.

For Muslims, the Qur'an is continuous with the Old and New Testaments: "We have made a covenant with the Israelites [and] you shall not be guided until you observe the Torah and the Gospel" (Q 5:70, 68). However, Muslims regard these two testaments as sharing a defect from which the Qur'an is free. For them, the Old and New Testaments were partially corrupted in transmission and have validity only when they confirm what the Qur'an maintains. When the three scriptures differ, the inerrancy of the Qur'an prevails. The Qur'an itself makes this explicit when it states: "This is the Scripture in which there is no doubt" (Q 2:2).

The belief that the Qur'an is literally the Word and words of God underscores the place of the Qur'an in the lives of Muslims. For them, it is God's guidance for all life, for all people, for all time. It regulates and evaluates every event. It is a reminder of daily doings as well as a repository of revealed truth. It is a road map for the will as well as a collection of sayings to meditate on in order to deepen our sense of God's glory. "Perfect are the words of thy Lord in truthfulness and justice" (Q 6:115). This explains in part why the Qur'an is the most recited book in the world. Certainly it is the world's most memorized book.

As we recall, the central affirmation of the Qur'an is the unity of God: "Know that there is no god but God and seek forgiveness for your sin" (Q 47:19); "You have no other God but He" (Q 11:61). In this the Qur'an is at one with the Old Testament, and indeed the words used there are almost identical to those used in, for example, Isaiah:

> Turn to me and be saved,
>   all the ends of the earth!
> For I am God and there is no other (45:22).

> Remember this and consider,
>   recall it to mind, you transgressors, . . .
> for I am God, and there is no other;
>   I am God and there is no one like me (46:8-9).

To reinforce its message, the Qur'an uses material found in the Old Testament. The accounts of Adam, Abraham, Moses, and many others are referred to as examples of those who proclaimed the message of monotheism.

When the Qur'an describes the nature of God, God is presented as both transcendent and immanent. God's transcendence is clear when God is described as the omnipotent Creator of the world (Q 35:1-2; 2:109), the Master of the Day of Doom (Q 1:3), who, as in the Psalms (139; 11:4), is a judge who sees all and knows all: "He is with you wherever you are; and God sees the things you do" (Q 57:4).

Two of the greatest Qur'anic statements about God emphasize God's transcendence:

> God—there is no god but He, the Living, the Everlasting. Slumber seizes Him not, neither sleep; to Him belongs all that is in the heavens and the earth. Who is there that shall intercede with Him save by his leave? He knows what lies before them and what is after them, and they comprehend not anything of His knowledge save such as

He wills. His Throne comprises the heavens and the earth; the preserving of them oppresses Him not; He is the All-high, the All-glorious (Q 2:255).

And:

He is God; there is no god but He. He is the knower of the Unseen and the Visible. He is the All-merciful, the All-compassionate. He is God; there is no god but He. He is the King, the All-holy, the All-peaceable, the All-faithful, the All-preserver, the All-mighty, the All-compeller, the All-sublime. Glory be to God, above that they associate! He is God, the Creator, the Maker, the Shaper. To Him belong the Names Most Beautiful. All that is in the Heavens and the earth magnifies Him; He is the All-mighty, the All-wise (Q 59:22-24).

Perhaps the best biblical parallel to the transcendent picture of God in the Qur'an is the last chapter of the book of Job, where Job acknowledges his insignificance in comparison with the greatness and majesty of God.

In the Qur'an, though God is transcendent and above all similitude, God is also immanent. God is not an indifferent, remote ruler of the universe. God in God's immanence is forever taking the first step toward men and women to draw them to Godself. The words "adore and draw nigh" were the last words uttered by the voice in the very first revelation (Q 96:19). Elsewhere we are told that every godly act that human beings perform is preceded by an act of God's favor toward them. In referring to backsliders who repented, the Qur'an says: "He turned towards them, that they might also turn; surely God turns, and is All-compassionate" (Q 9:119).

It is not surprising that the two most common attributes for God in the Qur'an are "Merciful and Compassionate." In fact, every chapter of the Qur'an, with the exception of chapter 9, begins with the formula: "In the Name of God, the Merciful, the Compassionate." These epithets used to describe God also can be found in the Old Testament. For example, Sirach 2:11 refers to God as "compassionate and merciful," as does the prayer of Manasseh in 2 Chronicles 30:9.

The message of the Qur'an is filled with joy and hope. It speaks not only of ultimate justice on the Day of Judgement, but also of help along the way and pardon for the contrite:

By the white forenoon and the brooding night! Thy Lord has neither forsaken thee nor hates thee and the Last shall be better for thee than the First. Thy Lord shall give thee, and thou shalt be satisfied. Did He not find thee an orphan, and shelter thee? Did He not find thee erring, and guide thee? Did he not find thee needy, and suffice thee? (Q 93:1-8).

A believer can at any time lift heart and soul into the presence of God to receive strength and guidance for life's troubled journey:

> We indeed created man; and We know what his soul whispers within him, and We are nearer to him than the jugular vein (Q 50:15).

The Qur'an teaches that people can come to a knowledge of God by considering God's works and contemplating God's creation:

> Surely in the creation of the heavens and the earth and the alternation of night and day and the ship that runs in the sea with profit to men, and the water God sends down from heaven therewith reviving the earth after it is dead and His scattering abroad in it all manner of crawling things, and the turning about of the winds and the clouds compelled between heaven and earth—surely there are signs for a people having understanding (Q 2:159).

If anyone wishes to know God, one has only to "journey through the earth and see how He hath brought forth created things" (Q 29:19). "Whithersoever you turn, there is the Face of God" (Q 2:109).

Paul makes the same claim when he says that ever since the creation of the world God's "eternal power and divine nature, invisible though they are, have been understood and seen through the things he has made" (Rom 1:20). And in the Psalms we read:

> The heavens are telling the glory of God,
>   and the firmament proclaims his handiwork.
>   (Ps 19:1)

The human response to God should be that of praise, love and service: "And proclaim the praise of thy Lord in the night, and at the declining of the stars" (Q 52:48-49). For

> hast thou not seen how that whatsoever is in the heavens and in the earth extols God, and the birds spreading their wings? Each—He knows its prayer and its extolling: and God knows the things they do. To God belongs the Kingdom of the heavens and the earth, and to Him, is the homecoming (Q 24:41-42).

To love God fully is to surrender to God totally. One who surrenders to God not only believes in God's message but also tries to live according to it, well aware that God is present in every place and time and that there is really no profane sphere of life. For such a person, not only prayer, but also the practice of mercy and justice is an essential part of true religion:

It is not piety, that you turn your faces to the East and to the West. True piety is this: to believe in God, and the Last Day, the angels, the Book, and the Prophets, to give of one's substance, however cherished, to kinsmen, and orphans, the needy, the traveller, beggars, and to ransom the slave, to perform the prayer, to pay the alms. And they who fulfil their covenant, and endure with fortitude misfortune, hardship and peril, these are they who are true in their faith, these are the truly godfearing (Q 2:172).

ISLAMIC LAW

After Muhammad immigrated to Yathrib/Medina, his message, as recorded in the Qur'an, began to include legislative, or legal, material pertaining to the ordering of life in the new supra-tribal religious community. About 10 percent of the Qur'an falls into this category. The inclusion of legal material in a revelation from God has its parallel in many books of the Old Testament.

After Muhammad's death, as Islam expanded out of Arabia, law continued to evolve and to play a central role in the unification of the Muslim world. In Islam this legal guidance is known as the *shari'a*, the Arabic word for "path" as it appears in Qur'an 45:18.

In the evolution of Islamic law, or the *shari'a*, the first foundation was the Qur'an. Upon this foundation legal experts developed three further principles that, together with the Qur'an, came to be known as the four foundations of the *shari'a*. These were the *sunna* (custom), *ijma* (consensus), and *qiyas* (analogy).

The second foundation of the *shari'a*, the *sunna*, is the record of the custom of Muhammad as opposed to the diverse local customs found in the expanding Islamic empire. This record takes the form of a collection of sayings concerning what Muhammad said and did. Each saying is called a *hadith*. Thus the *hadith* is the vehicle of the *sunna*. There are six collections of *hadiths* commonly recognized as sound by most Muslims.

The justification for regarding the *hadiths* as an authoritative source of divine guidance comes from the Qur'an: "Obey God and the prophet" (Q 33:33; 4:58); "Truly in the messenger of God you have a beautiful model" (Q 33:21). In many respects the Christian analogy to the *hadiths* is the New Testament, which records what Jesus said and did.

The third foundation of Islamic law, *ijma,* or the consensus of the community, in turn lies in a *hadith* attributed to Muhammad: "My community will not agree on error." This *hadith* was taken to justify the view that if at any time in the history of Islam the community came to a consensus on a question about which neither the Qur'an nor the *sunna* made any specific statement, that consensus became part of the *shari'a*. This idea is not unlike the Roman Catholic notion of *sensus fidelium*, the sense of the faithful, which is recognized as a guide in living the faith.

The fourth foundation of the *shari'a*, *qiyas* (analogy), was introduced to deal with new legal problems and issues. Its aim was to limit the use of personal opinion by suggesting that sound guidance could come only through reasoning by analogy with existing points of law, somewhat like what lawyers in the West call argument from precedent.

The development and codification of Islamic law took place within the first three centuries after the death of Muhammad. In theory, its four foundations—the Qur'an, the *sunna* (custom), *ijma* (consensus), and *qiyas* (analogy)—provide a comprehensive system of divine guidance for Muslims in all areas of private and public life, including the organization of the state and relationships between communities and nations. It is possible to say that the achievement of legal scholars in early Islam is comparable to that of the church fathers in early Christianity. They affirmed what they considered to be the authoritative viewpoint against deviating tendencies.

SUNNIS AND SHI'ITES

Muslims accept the *shari'a* as the manifestation of God's compassionate love for the world and a means by which the unity of God can be reflected in the unity of all human life. This is the Islamic ideal, just as in Christianity there is the ideal of one church, one faith, one God. In actuality, both religious communities are divided.

In Islam the major division is between Sunni and Shi'i Muslims. The division came about as follows: After Muhammad's death, Muslims were not in agreement concerning the temporal leadership of the community. One group maintained that Muhammad had designated Ali, his cousin and son-in-law, and Ali's descendants to be his successors. This group came to be called the *shi'a* ("party," "faction") of Ali, popularly known as Shi'ites.

The other group, convinced that Muhammad had done no such thing, opted for choosing a leader from a group of elder associates of Muhammad. This group came to be called "People of the Sunna and the Assembly," Sunnis for short. They elected Abu Bakr, one of the first persons to embrace Islam in Mecca, as the first caliph or successor to Muhammad. When Abu Bakr led the community (632-34), followed by Umar (634-44) and Uthman (644-56), Ali's supporters continued to insist that Ali had been unfairly passed over three times. Finally, Ali was elected the fourth caliph in 656.

Five years after the death of Ali the community became even more divided. The Shi'ites argued for continuing leadership in the family of Muhammad through his two grandsons, Hasan and Husayn. However, the majority favored Mu'awiya, the governor of Syria, who was caliph from

661 to 680. The disagreement festered and erupted into conflict. In 680, in the battle of Karbala, a city in Iraq, Husayn was murdered by troops of Yazid, Mu'awiya's son and successor. Viewing the death of Husayn as that of a martyr, the Shi'ites dissociated themselves from the main body of the Muslims, the Sunnis, and formed a distinct community within Islam.

What began as a question of succession soon acquired a religious character. The Shi'ites called those whom they considered to be the legitimate successors to Muhammad Imams instead of caliphs, as the Sunnis did. However, while they adhered to their belief that a true successor to Muhammad must be of the family of the prophet, many sects developed among them over disputes centered on the right to succession of the fifth, seventh, and twelfth Imams. They rejected the first three Imams of the Sunnis and regarded the fourth caliph Ali as the first Imam. Hasan (d. 669) and Husayn (d. 680), Ali's two sons, became the second and third Imams. After the death of Husayn, his son Ali Zayn al-Abedin (d. 712) became the fourth Imam. He had two sons, Zayd (d. 740) and Muhammad al-Baqir (d. 731). Zaydi Shi'ites recognized Zayd as the fifth and final Imam. Other Shi'ites acknowledged his brother as the fifth Imam. Al-Baqir's son, Ja'fir al-Sadiq (d. 765), became the sixth Imam. He in turn had two sons, Isma'il (d. 760) and Musa al-Kazim (d. 799). Isma'ili or Sevener Shi'ites contended that Isma'il was the rightful seventh and last Imam. Other Shi'i groups supported Musa al-Kazim. Twelver Shi'ites continued to recognize the line of succession through Musa al-Kazim to Muhammad al-Muntazar, the twelfth and final Imam, who disappeared in the year 878 and is expected some day to return.

Twelver Shi'ites make up the main body of Shi'ism in the Islamic world today. They believe that Muhammad imparted part of his teaching directly to Ali, and through him to the subsequent Imams. Thus to the four foundations of the *shari'a* recognized by Sunnis, they add a fifth, the teaching of the Imams.

Since the disappearance of Muhammad al-Muntazar, actual leadership of the Twelver Shi'i community has been conducted by *ulema* (the Arabic word for "teachers/scholars"). The representative of the (Hidden) Imam is called a *marja' al-taqlid* and his interpretation of the religious law is binding on all Twelver Shi'ites. Under him there is a kind of religious hierarchy with *mullahs* (the Persian word for "teachers") at the lowest level and *ayatollahs* at the highest level of authority. The rise to power of Khomeini through the 1979 revolution in Iran was facilitated by the fact that he was a *marja' al-taqlid.*

In the development of a religious hierarchy Shi'ites departed from the basic egalitarian outlook of the Sunnis. James A. Bill and John Alden Williams observe that the religious hierarchy of the Shi'ites has its parallel in Roman Catholicism.[2] For them, the egalitarian outlook of the Sunni *ulema* has its parallel in the Protestant churches.

There is a similarity between Shi'ism and Roman Catholicism concerning the deaths of Husayn and Jesus, for just as Shi'ites regard the death of Husayn as that of a martyr so do Roman Catholics view the death of Jesus on the cross. Moreover, Bill and Williams point out, "In both cases, the drama of suffering and the legend of martyrdom have been institutionalized and remain living, integral parts of the system of faith."[3] They elaborate on the similarity when they add:

> In Shi'ism and Catholicism alike, the passion and deaths of Christ and Imam Husayn are commemorated every day of every year. In Catholicism, this daily commemoration is of course the mass. In addition, yearly during the Lenten season (and especially during Holy Week, and, paramountly, Good Friday), Christ's crucifixion and death are a profound spiritual event in the life of the practicing Roman Catholic. Likewise in Shi'ism, the death of Imam Husayn at Karbala is vividly recalled throughout the year, in Shi'i mosques, prayer sessions and devotional readings, while the commemorative mourning is dramatized each year in the first ten days of the month of Muharram [the first month of the Muslim calendar]. The actual death of Imam Husayn is recalled on Ashura [the tenth day], and the entire period is marked by passion plays, mourning ceremonies, fasting, and prayer recitations of profound grief. . . . Holy Week as practiced by Catholics is not unlike the ten days of Muharram as commemorated by Shi'is.[4]

Today Twelver Shi'ites represent more than 90 percent of the population of Iran, the only country in the Islamic world in which Shi'i Islam is the state religion. They form slightly more than 50 percent of Iraq. The Twelver population of Lebanon is about 30 percent. In the Indian subcontinent they make up some 10 to 15 percent of the Muslim population. In total, 10 to 15 percent of the world's Muslims are Shi'i. The vast majority of the remaining 85 to 90 percent are Sunni.

SUFISM

Sufism is not a Muslim sect, but rather the name given to the mysticism of Islam. Just as Christian monasticism evolved as a reaction against some of the trends toward worldliness that had emerged when Christianity became the official religion of the Roman Empire in the fourth century, so Sufism emerged in part as a protest against the worldliness that the Sufis saw as overtaking Islam once Muslims became powerful through their early conquests.

The term *Sufism* probably is derived from the Arabic word for wool (*suf*), since the Sufis, the early ascetics of Islam, wore coarse woollen garments—in contrast to the silks and satins of the opulent—to symbolize their rejection of the world. These ascetics are also known as "the poor," *al-fuqara'*, the plural of *faqir*, in Persian *darvish*, whence the English words *fakir* and *dervish*. The poverty of the Sufis was not a mere lack of wealth but the lack of the desire for wealth: the empty hand as well as the empty heart. Their poverty was in keeping with the beatitude of Jesus: "Blessed are the poor in spirit, for theirs is the kingdom of heaven" (Mt 5:3).

Islamic law teaches that every Muslim can bear witness to the unity of God by submitting to its decrees. Sufism requires that this witness should be not merely a form of lip service, or even a mental assent, but a witness born of an intuitive and immediate experience of God.

To bear such witness calls for detachment from the ego. As Titus Burckhardt, a contemporary Sufi, observes:

> God can only be known . . . when the human ego, which instinctively regards itself as a self-sufficient centre—a kind of 'divinity' in addition to the Divinity—is extinguished before the infinitude of God, in accordance with the words: "There is no divinity but God." This does not mean that the immortal essence of the soul has to be annihilated; what must be dissolved is that mental morass, compounded of ego-determined passions and imaginings, the constant tendency of which is to restrict consciousness to the level of ephemeral appearances. When this "veil" of selfishness is lifted from the Spirit which is hidden underneath—the Spirit which sees through to the essences of things—then for the first time things are seen as they really are. God is seen in His all-embracing Presence, and the creature as a pure possibility contained in the Divine Being.[5]

Put another way, for Sufis, God cannot be known by the senses, for God is immaterial; not by the intellect, for God is unthinkable; not by logic, for logic never gets beyond the finite; not by book-learning, for book-learning fosters conceit and obscures the truth of God with clouds of empty words.[6] The Persian mystic Jalaluddin Rumi (1207-73) asks theologians:

> Do you know a name without a thing answering
> to it?
> Have you ever plucked a rose from R, O, S, E?
> You name His name; go, seek the reality named
> by it.
> Look for the moon in the sky, not in the water!
> If you desire to rise above mere names and
> letters,
> Make yourself free from self at one stroke.
> Become pure from all attributes of self,
> That you may see your own bright essence,

> Yea, see in your own heart the knowledge of the
> Prophet,
> Without book, without tutor, without preceptor.[7]

For Sufis, knowledge of God comes through direct intuitive experiences through which they taste and see the goodness of their God.

In the Sufi approach to God there are three stages: the purgative, the contemplative, and the unitive.[8] The purgative stage is a time to repent and seek forgiveness for our sins and to amend our lives. The need for purgation has its roots in the Qur'an: "Be patient, then, for the promise of God is true. Seek forgiveness for your sin and occupy yourself in the praise of your Lord" (Q 40:55; also 47:19; 11:61; 27:45-46). Purgation calls for the purification of our being by the elimination of all those qualities and attitudes that separate us from God, that subject us to the dominance of our ego and of outer things. Pride, anger, self-love, and self-assertion must be renounced. The detachment from the ego that comes through purgation is the work of God, though it demands a certain cooperation on our part: "Whosoever shall strive for Our sake, We will guide into Our ways" (Q 29:69).

Purgation constrains the will toward purity of heart and fills the soul with a passionate longing to be united with God. In Sufi mystical writing this longing has been likened to

> a moaning dove that has lost its mate; to a reed torn from its bed and made into a flute whose plaintive music fills the eyes with tears; to a falcon summoned by the fowler's whistle to perch upon his wrist; to snow melting in the sun and mounting as vapour to the sky; to a frenzied camel plunging through the desert by night; to a caged parrot, a fish on dry land, a pawn that seeks to become a king.[9]

The longing of the soul for God leads to the stage of contemplation. To progress in contemplation, the Sufis recognized the need for solitude to deal with distractions from the outside world, following the example of the Prophet Muhammad in his frequent retreats to Mount Hira.

Withdrawn from the noise and cares of the world, the Sufis made a practice of repeating the name of God or some short religious formula such as "Glory to God," "There is no god but God," accompanying the repetition with an intense concentration of every faculty upon the single word or phrase.

The impetus for this practice, called *dhikr* ("remembrance"), is derived from those Qur'anic verses that enjoin on every Muslim the practice of remembering God often (Q 33:41), for the peaceful heart is one in which the remembrance of God has become second nature (Q 13:28-29).

The practice of *dhikr* involves rhythmic breathing and an attempt to turn the five senses inward. Introspection results in distractions from within as the remembrance of God and God's promises competes with the remembrance of the life of the ego in a battle for the soul.

Since it is by dying to oneself that one lives for God, one gets rid of distractions by concentrating on God alone. When the will is surrendered to God and the mind is concentrated on God alone, the soul moves from a discursive to an intuitive mode of knowing, in which one can no longer distinguish between the one remembering and the Remembered. This state of total self-forgetfulness is called *fana*.[10] Self-forgetfulness leads to a sudden and direct knowledge of God. While ordinary knowledge is denoted by the term *'ilm*, Sufis call the direct knowledge of God *ma'rifat*.[11] It is not the result of any mental process. It is the light of God that flashes into the heart and overwhelms every human faculty with its dazzling beams. Direct knowledge of God comes through an experience that is ineffable—beyond words, beyond thought, beyond all conceiving. He who knows God is dumb.

Jesus is an important figure in Sufism. Though all Muslims regard Muhammad as the "seal of Prophecy," some Sufis refer to Jesus as the "Seal of Sanctity." The famous Spanish Sufi Muhyi al-Din Ibn 'Arabi (1165-1240) was one of them. In his celebrated *Al-Futuhat al-Makkiya (The Meccan Revelations)*, he had this to say on the matter:

> The Seal of universal holiness, above which there is no other holy, is our Lord Jesus. We have met several contemplatives of the heart of Jesus. . . . I myself have been united to him several times in my ecstasies, and by his ministry I returned to God at my conversion. . . . He has given me the name of friend and has prescribed austerity and nakedness of spirit.[12]

And, indeed, there are parallels in the Bible and the Christian tradition to the Sufi praxis of spirituality. In biblical spirituality, as in Sufism, spiritual vision calls for self-denial and detachment from the ego. We must put to death what is earthly in us—"immorality, impurity, passion, evil desire and covetousness, which is idolatry" (Col 3:5; also Rom 6:12; Ti 2:12; 1 Pt 2:11, 4:2); mortify the body and crucify the flesh (Rom 8:13; Gal 5:24); prefer the good of others before our own (Lk 3:11; Rom 14:20-21; 15:1-2; 1 Cor 10:24, 33; 13:5; Phil 2:4); put off our old nature, which belongs to our former manner of life, and put on the new nature, created in the likeness of God in true righteousness and holiness (Eph 4:22; Col 3:9); be crucified to the world (Gal 6:14), and not love the things that are in it (1 Jn 2:15); and forsake all (Lk 14:33), even lawful things (1 Cor 10:23).

In the Bible, as in Sufism, true knowledge of God is experiential in character. It is the revelation of the mystery of God (1 Cor 2:6ff.), which God gives to those who have faith in God (1 Cor 2:10-16; 12:8). Believers know, because God dwells in them (Jn 14:7) and transforms them into

God's likeness (1 Jn 3:2). Those who have this knowledge know the truth, and truth sets them free from sin (Jn 8:31-32). It is a blessed vision that is the fruit of a perfect life lived in and for God. As the beatitudes state: "Blessed are the pure in heart, for they will see God" (Mt 5:8). Knowing is the result of becoming one and being one with God through love: "Everyone who loves is born of God. . . . Whoever does not love does not know God, for God is love" (1 Jn 4:7-8).

In the Bible, as in Sufism, the ascent to God calls for purgation. To have true knowledge of God we need to be converted to God, for only God is able to lead us to God's own wisdom (1 Cor 2:10-13). God comes to meet us in love and forgiveness, but there must first be true repentance. We find this teaching in the preaching of John the Baptist (Mk 1:4) and in the ministry of Jesus. When Jesus came into Galilee his first message to his hearers was that they should repent (Mk 1:15). And doubtless Paul had some purgative discipline in mind when he said, "Be transformed by the renewing of your minds" (Rom 12:2), and exhorted us to train ourselves in godliness (1 Tm 4:7).

The Bible, like Sufism, recognizes that purgation prepares the soul for contemplation, and that to progress in contemplation, one must free oneself from mundane distractions. In the Old Testament God takes Hosea into solitude to hedge up all the ways he used to run after the desires and thoughts of the world (Hos 2:6). Moses retires to the wilderness to better commune with God (Ex 18:5; 19; 34:27-28), as does Elijah (1 Kgs 17:3-6). In the New Testament, too, Paul (Gal 1:17), John the Baptist (Mt 3:1-6), and Jesus himself (Mt 4:1-2) go into the desert to be alone. Contemplative prayer has to be inward, and this calls for discipline. Hence the advice of Jesus to his disciples: "Whenever you pray, go into your room and shut the door and pray to your Father who is secret" (Mt 6:6).

The Bible, like Sufism, acknowledges that attention to one's breathing can help to dispel distractions from within, so that the breath of God which brings understanding (Jb 32:8) can be heard as soft and light as an exhalation (1 Kgs 19:12).

The Bible, like Sufism, recognizes that the repetition of the name of God or some short phrase is an effective method of contemplation:

> The name of the LORD is a strong tower;
> the righteous run into it and are safe.
> (Prv 18:10)

> Everyone who calls on the name of the Lord
> shall be saved (Acts 2:21).

A fourteenth-century Catholic mystic explains this method of concentration in *The Cloud of Unknowing*:

If you want to gather all your desire into one simple word that the mind can easily retain, choose a short word rather than a long one. A one-syllable word such as "God" or "love" is best. But choose one that is meaningful to you. Then fix it in your mind so that it will remain there come what may. . . . Use it to beat upon the cloud of darkness above you and subdue all distractions, consigning them to the cloud of forgetting beneath you. Should some thought go on annoying you, demanding to know what you are doing, answer it with this word alone. If your mind begins to intellectualize over the meaning and connotations of this little word, remind yourself that its value lies in its simplicity. Do this and I assure you that these thoughts will vanish. Why? Because you have refused to develop them with arguing.[13]

In the history of Christian spirituality John Cassian (360?-432?) was the first person to describe this practice of repetition, which he learned from the desert fathers. He does so in chapter 10 of his Tenth Conference, one of the most beautiful passages in Christian writing, using this verse: "Come to my help, O God; Lord, hurry to my rescue."[14] John Climacus (579-649) attaches particular importance to the repetition of the Jesus prayer.[15] Later the standard form of this prayer, "Lord Jesus Christ, Son of God, have mercy on me," was widely practiced in the monasteries of Mount Athos. This prayer combined with respiratory discipline became the soul of the Hesychast movement in the thirteenth century[16] and in recent centuries has spread widely among the Orthodox churches, whence comes that little gem of a book *The Way of a Pilgrim*.[17]

A similar method of deepening concentration appears both in the repetition of the Hail Mary in the Rosary and in Gregorian chants. In all these examples from Sufism and Christianity, repetition is a way of restricting reflective consciousness. It is a method for warding off discursive reasoning, thinking, and conceptualization. It narrows the horizon of rational consciousness and prepares the mind for a breakthrough into intuitive consciousness.

In the Bible, as in Sufism, distractions cease when we reach a state of complete self-forgetfulness *(fana)* through concentration on God alone. Self-forgetfulness clears the way for entrance into the intuitive way of knowing God beyond the normal conventions of thought. This stage brings to mind the sayings of Jesus that "those who find their life will lose it" (Mt 10:39) and "unless a grain of wheat falls into the earth and dies, it remains just a single grain; but if it dies, it bears much fruit" (Jn 12:24).

The prohibition of images of God enjoined at Mount Sinai goes well beyond images engraved on stone or wood to include our words and concepts. Isaiah's confession of God's hiddenness implies that God lies beyond the range of the intellect (Is 45:15). Paul makes the same point when he says that God dwells in "unapproachable light" (1 Tm 6:16) and when he tells us that any experience of God "surpasses all understanding" (Phil 4:7). For Paul, to be morbidly concerned over mere verbal questions and quibbles leads us to lose our grasp of the truth (1 Tm 6:5). He, and Jeremiah, go as far as to say that clinging to images of God is an impediment to finding the living God and is a form of idolatry (Rom 1:23; Jer 2:11). To encounter God, we must be still and let God be God (Ps 46:10).

In the Bible, as in the Sufi understanding of *ma'rifat*, the direct knowledge and vision of God comes suddenly: "The Lord spoke suddenly to Moses" (Nm 12:4), and on the road to Damascus "a great light from heaven suddenly shone about [Saul]" (Acts 22:6). The direct experience of God, whenever it appears, is ineffable. When Jeremiah encounters God directly, he does not know how to speak (Jer 1:6). When Paul is "caught up into Paradise," he is unable to say what happened to him (2 Cor 12:3). As we have seen, the spiritual ascent to God is similar in the Bible and in Sufism.

Because Sufis gathered around spiritual masters *(shaykhs)*, forming circles that crystallized into religious orders *(tariqas)*, it is possible to liken the Sufi orders to the contemplative orders in the Roman Catholic Church, with the difference that Sufis generally marry. Sufi orders, like Catholic contemplative orders, generally insisted that their members refrain from work in the world. However, the Shadhilyah order, named after its founder, Abu Hasan al-Shadhili (1196-1258), wanted his followers to work in the secular world. The *Kitab al-Hikam (Book of Wisdom)* of Ibn 'Ata' Allah (d. 1309),[18] the third *shaykh* of the order, epitomizes this emphasis in the order's spirituality. In this respect, as Peter J. Awn has pointed out, the *shaykhs* of the Shadhilyah order

> were precursors of a similar development in the Christian West, when, in the sixteenth century, Ignatius of Loyola founded the Society of Jesus, or Jesuits, whose members, contrary to the traditional monastic structures, were intent on fostering *contemplatio in actione*, contemplation while remaining fully involved in the secular world. Ibn 'Ata' Allah's *Hikam* has a place of honor in Islamic spirituality equal to that of Loyola's *Spiritual Exercises* in Christianity.[19]

An examination of Ibn 'Ata' Allah's *Kitab al-Hikam* and Ignatius Loyola's *Spiritual Exercises* would require a book in itself and so is beyond the scope of this introduction. However, a brief comparison of Ignatius's *Spiritual Exercises* and the spiritual exercises of Sufis in general still makes Awn's observation quite intriguing. For Ignatius, as for the Sufis, to know God it is necessary for us to abandon our own will and to make it correspond to the divine will. The very title *Spiritual Exercises* indicates this: "We call Spiritual Exercises every way of preparing and disposing the soul to rid itself from all inordinate attachments" (*SE* 1,

21).[20] For Ignatius, spiritual exercises are necessary because of the disorder of the human heart. Our "inordinate attachments" (*SE* 1), "the disorder" of our actions (*SE* 63), and "worldly love" (*SE* 97) deprive us of inner freedom to serve God alone.

Hence Ignatius makes detachment from the ego the very principle and foundation of his *Spiritual Exercises*: "Therefore, we must make ourselves indifferent to all created things. . . . Our one desire and choice should be to what is more conducive to the end for which we are created" (*SE* 23). The degree of our detachment from the ego is the degree of our attachment to God. Total detachment leads to union with God, and this is the goal.

To develop detachment Ignatius, like the Sufis, introduces us to the purgative way (*SE* 10) when he states that exercitants should begin the Exercises with a consideration and contemplation of sin (*SE* 4). He expects exercitants to attack the roots of their personal sins by getting to know the slightest disorder in themselves. He expects them to desire "a deep knowledge of [their] sins and a feeling of abhorrence for them; an understanding of the disorder of [their] actions, that filled with horror of them, they may amend their life and put it in order" (*SE* 63). Toward this end he advises them to recall the sins of their past life (*SE* 56). Elsewhere he instructs exercitants to enter the Exercises "with magnanimity and generosity," offering God "their entire will and liberty" and the disposition of their person (*SE* 5). He insists that people "must keep in mind that in all that concerns the spiritual life [their] progress will be in proportion to [their] surrender of self love, and of [their] own will and interests" (*SE* 189).

For Ignatius, as for Sufis, purgation prepares the soul for contemplation. Like the Sufis, he recognizes the need for solitude in contemplative prayer and makes much of withdrawing from the distractions of the world to make the soul more fit to approach and be united with God (*SE* 20).

In his second and third methods of prayer Ignatius, like Sufis, recognizes that the repetition of a single word or phrase, coordinated with one's breathing, is an effective method of contemplation (*SE* 252 and 258). The repetition helps to turn the senses inward. The distractions from within during concentration come from the ego, because of the craving for "sensual delights and gratifications" (*SE* 314), our "inclination to what is low and earthly" (*SE* 317), or "because we have been tepid, slothful, or negligent in our exercises of piety" (*SE* 322).

For Ignatius, as for Sufis, as concentration deepens, distractions cease and we enter a state of complete self-forgetfulness (*fana*). With self-forgetfulness there is a progressive deepening from the discursive mode of knowing to the non-discursive and intuitive. As he explains in *SE* 50, for example, one practices reflection on the subject matter of contemplation so that the will may move the affections to a way of knowing beyond the intellect. That is, a simpler and deeper interiority leads to higher spiritual perceptions and an experiential knowledge of the truth. That is the aim of all contemplation, for as Ignatius explains, "It is not so much knowledge which fills and satisfies the soul, but rather the interior understanding of and relish of the truth" (*SE* 2).

For Ignatius, as for Sufis, contemplation should lead to a mystical union with God, a state in which the soul embraces divine things without any intervening agency. He seems to imply that this state of the soul is the supreme end of prayer when he refers to a soul finding its Creator and Lord in a "consolation without previous cause" (*SE* 330 and 336). There is "direct" contact; God inflames the soul with "his love and praise" (*SE* 15; also 20), enabling it to "taste the infinite sweetness of divinity" (*SE* 124).

Ignatius describes this state of soul in his famous letter to Sister Teresa Rejadell:

It frequently happens that our Lord moves and urges the soul to this or that activity. He begins by enlightening the soul; that is to say, by speaking interiorly to it without the din of words, lifting it up wholly to his divine love and ourselves to his meaning without any possibility of resistance on our part, even should we wish to resist.[21]

The letter's wordless experience ("without the din of words") means that it is an experience "without concepts," "without particular objects of thought."[22] Like *ma'rifat* in Sufism, a direct knowledge of God comes through a sudden, ineffable experience of the divine.

Our reflection on Sufism and biblical and Christian spirituality has shown that Christians and Muslims agree that for religion to be personally authentic it must involve some direct religious experience and not be merely an affirmation of propositions accepted on the basis of authority—a teaching that seems to be alluded to in the epistle of James. Moreover, in spite of certain denials, the reflection makes it clear that for both Christians and Muslims a personal, direct experience of the ground of our salvation requires some kind of prior discipline to establish oneself in silence, not just physical silence but a silence of the senses, a silence of the mind, until that silence is reached for which there is no word.

Building on this introduction to Muhammad and the people who try to live by his message, chapter 2 will focus on the cultural, political, and economic obstacles to the Christian-Muslim dialogue.

Questions for Discussion

1. How is the Islamic account of Muhammad's call to prophethood reminiscent of the call of many Old Testament prophets?

2. Since some Old Testament prophets engaged in war and politics, should Muhammad's participation in these matters cast doubt on the authenticity of his prophethood?

3. Compare the conception of God found in the Old Testament with that found in the Qur'an.

4. What is the proper human response to God in the Qur'an and in the Old Testament?

5. What is the proper human response to God in the Qur'an and in the New Testament?

6. How does the Christian understanding of the place of law in religion differ from the Muslim understanding?

7. Does the inclusion of legal material in the Qur'an in itself establish that it is not a revelation from God?

8. Is there any similarity in the way the Muslim and Christian communities became divided?

9. How do Sunnis differ from Shi'ites?

10. Are there any similarities between Shi'ism and Roman Catholicism?

11. In the Sufi approach to God, what are the stages through which one must pass to have a direct experience of God? Are there parallels to these states in the Bible? In the Christian tradition?

Suggested Readings

Ali, Syed Ameer. *The Spirit of Islam*. London: Methuen, 1965.

Arberry, A. J. *Sufism*. New York: Harper & Row, 1970.

Awn, Peter J. "Sufism." Pages 104-22. In *The Encyclopedia of Religion*. Volume 13. Edited by Mircea Eliade. New York: Macmillan, 1987.

Esposito, John L. *Islam: The Straight Path*. New York: Oxford University Press, 1991.

Goddard, Hugh. *Christians and Muslims: From Double Standards to Mutual Understanding*. Richmond, Surrey: Curzon Press, 1995.

Goldziher, Ignaz. *Introduction to Islamic Theology and Law*. Princeton: Princeton University Press, 1981.

Martinson, Paul Varo, ed. *Islam: An Introduction for Christians.* Minneapolis: Augsburg, 1994.

Nasr, Seyyed Hussein. *Ideals and Realities of Islam.* Boston: Beacon Press, 1966.

Nicholson, Reynold A. *The Mystics of Islam.* London: Routledge and Kegan Paul, 1975.

Pickthall, Muhammad. *The Meaning of the Glorious Koran.* New York: New American Library, 1953.

Rahman, Fazlur. *Major Themes of the Qur'an.* Chicago: Bibliotheca Islamica, 1980.

Sherif, Faruq. *A Guide to the Contents of the Qur'an.* Reading, UK: Ithaca Press, 1995.

Watt, W. Montgomery. *Bell's Introduction to the Qur'an.* Edinburgh: Edinburgh University Press, 1970.

—————. *Muhammad: Prophet and Statesman.* London: Oxford University Press, 1961.

2

The Historical Background

CHRISTIANITY BEFORE ISLAM

The attempt of Alexander the Great (356-23 B.C.E.) to integrate the Middle East into his vast empire by imposing Greek culture on its peoples set the stage for tensions between Christianity and Islam when these religions came into being at a later period. It all began when, in his eastward March, Alexander defeated the Persian army in 324 B.C.E. and swept all before him. Before his death in 323 B.C.E. Asia Minor, Syria, Palestine, Egypt, Mesopotamia, Iran, and India to the Indus had been conquered and brought into his empire. After his death his chief generals continued to battle for the empire, which they eventually divided. Following the breakup of the empire, the Middle East fell heir to a century of international political anarchy and intermittent wars. Yet this period was the apex of the brilliant Hellenistic Age, which persisted for two centuries more until the last vestige of Ptolemaic rule ended with Cleopatra's suicide in 30 B.C.E..[1]

After Cleopatra's death the Middle East became eastern provinces of the Roman Empire, which continued Alexander's policy to hellenize the Middle East. This policy was accelerated when the second century saw the rise and spread of Christianity in the Middle East. Because the church in the Eastern Roman Empire allied itself with Greek culture, the spread of Christianity occurred almost exclusively in the hellenized cities and provinces of the Roman Empire. Being a city religion that used the Greek language exclusively, "it exerted its influence only on the Hellenistic upper strata of society and never established a vitalizing contact with the tongues and ways of life of the ancient native cultures" of the indigenous peoples.[2] In other words, in the eastern provinces of the Roman Empire most people led a life without hellenism and, as a consequence, in the religious sphere, without Christianity.

More important, while a part of the hellenized upper strata of society accepted Christianity as it was presented to them, another part attempted to make an original synthesis of Oriental culture, hellenism, and Christianity. These attempts resulted in questionable formulations of Christian doctrine that centered on the Incarnation and the Trinity, among which Arianism, Nestorianism, and Monophysitism are the most important.

Language and culture played an important role in the disputes over the formulation of doctrine, since they were disputes between Christians, whose mother tongue was Greek, and Oriental Christians, whose native language was Syrian, Armenian, or Coptic. Though the Oriental Christians used Greek for theological discussions, "their thinking was essentially in the categories and concepts proper to the mentality associated with each language. Differences of mentality led to differences of theological formulation on various matters."[3] When the formulations of the Oriental Christians came before the ecumenical councils, they were outvoted by those whose first language was Greek.

The disputes between the Greek and Oriental Christians were complicated by the existence of Latin-speaking Christians. The formulation of the christological and trinitarian doctrine that the ecumenical councils eventually accepted was a compromise between Greek-speaking and Latin-speaking Christians. Though the Latin terms for the doctrine of the Trinity (one *substantia*, three *personae*) were not identical to the Greek terms (one *ousia*, three *hypostaseis*), since *substantia* corresponds etymologically to *hypostasis*, Latin- and Greek-speaking theologians agreed that the two sets of terms should be regarded as equivalent.[4] There was no formulation of trinitarian or christological doctrine recognized as being generally within the central Christian tradition expressed in the languages of the people of the Middle East. The agreed-upon formulations were Western. Thus the church failed to deal with the problem created by the different intellectual categories presupposed by those who spoke the Oriental languages. The failure to inculturate the faith in Middle Eastern culture, even before the birth of Muhammad, helped to prepare the way for the rise and spread of Islam.

The need to inculturate the faith in Middle Eastern culture disappeared when Constantine (d. 327) became emperor of both the Western and Eastern Roman Empires in 324. Faced with the challenge to unify both parts of the empire, he began an era that made use of force to achieve uniformity in the Christian faith by imposing the agreed-upon Western formulations of the faith on the multicultural society of the Middle East. Even though he was not baptized a Christian until he was on his deathbed, he dealt with the Arian dispute by convening and presiding over the first ecumenical council of the Christian church at Nicea in 325, and went as far as to have soldiers present at the council to ensure that the bishops reached agreement on the issue.[5] Constantine's action resulted in the interdependence of church and state, which is known as the *caesaropapism* of the Eastern Roman (or Byzantine) Empire. Needless to say, the symbiosis of church and state ensured the permanent alienation of the masses in the Middle East and helped to prepare the way for the rapid expansion of Islam four centuries later.

More concretely, the Arian dispute was named after Arius (c. 250-336), an Egyptian priest who rejected the teaching that the three persons of the Trinity are equal. He taught that the Son was inferior to the Father and that the Holy Spirit was inferior to both the Father and the Son. This descending triad negates the divinity of Christ and of the Holy Spirit and regards the Father alone as the true God. At the Council of Nicea, Constantine, "at the urging of his theological advisor Hosius of Cordova (d. 357), suggested that the Father and the Son were *homoousios*, of one substance (consubstantial)."[6] The council went along with the suggestion and condemned the Arian doctrine. Arius and his chief supporters were silenced and sent into exile.

Unfortunately, the Greek term *homoousios* is vague and "could be interpreted as saying that the Father and the Son are numerically one."[7] Because of this ambiguity, many bishops had reservations about Nicea, and after the council withdrew their support for the proclamation. And so Arianism continued to be a disputed question until Emperor Theodosius I (d. 395) called the Council of Constantinople in 381. This council ended the dispute and added the proviso that the Holy Spirit is *homoousios* with the Father and the Son. The Council of Constantinople also established Catholicism as the official religion of the Roman Empire. Faced with persecution, the supporters of the Arian doctrine soon disappeared from the Middle East.[8]

Just as Arianism impelled the church to clarify its trinitarian teaching, so Nestorianism impelled it to clarify its Christology. This came about when Nestorius (c. 381-451), born in Syria, was accused of teaching that Christ had two distinct natures embodied in two persons, one human and one divine; that Mary was not the mother of God, but had given birth only to the man Jesus; and that, consequently, only the man Jesus died on the cross. Emperor Theodosius II (d. 450) convoked the Council of Ephesus in 431 to deal with this dispute. The council condemned Nestorius, and persecution followed. The Nestorians took refuge in the Persian Empire, where they flourished.[9]

The condemnation of Nestorius did not settle the issue. Instead, it led to the next dispute, Monophysitism. If Nestorius had separated the divine and human natures in Christ, Eutyches (c. 378-454) eliminated the distinction, claiming that Christ had two natures before the incarnation but only one nature *(monophysis)* after it. The new doctrine was called the Monophysite doctrine, signifying that Jesus Christ had only one nature—the divine. Emperor Marcian (d. 457) convoked the Council of Chalcedon in 451 to settle the issue. This council condemned the Monophysite doctrine and affirmed that in Christ there is one person with two natures, one human and one divine. Savage persecution of the Monophysite Christians in Egypt, Palestine, Syria, Abyssinia, and Armenia followed.[10]

As we have seen, from Constantine to Marcian the Byzantine state embodied imperial tradition, Christian orthodoxy, and hellenistic culture.

The consequence was decisive for the future of Christianity. The ruthlessness with which the authority of the Byzantine state was applied in the interest of power politics and religion greatly enhanced the nationalistic separatism of the peoples of the Middle East. Soon hatred for their political oppressors was directed against official Christianity. Thus even before the birth of Islam people were always prepared to form alliances with any non-Christian power for the sake of liberating themselves from the religious domination of a church alien to them.

To complicate matters even further, the Byzantine Empire had a great rival, the Persian Empire. The rivalry between these two superpowers led to a series of wars, with only brief intervals of peace. The long-continued struggle of the giants had its repercussions in Arabia. The Persians had a sphere of influence on the eastern and southern coasts, while the Byzantine Empire had its sphere of influence on the western trade routes of the peninsula. Thus in the year 570, the year in which Muhammad was born, we find the Byzantines trying to gain control of Mecca, the very city in which Muhammad was born, and the Persians trying to gain control of Yemen in South Arabia.

The connection among religion, politics, and culture could not have escaped the notice of the Arabs, living as they were in a buffer state between the two superpowers. Moreover, at that time in history, no one thought it wrong for either power to use force to impose its supremacy over the nations of the Middle East. And so when Islam was born, "whether it liked it or not," it "could not but fit into its own period. The train was already moving; Islam had only to catch it."[11] Furthermore, "the charge of Christendom against Islam was that its doctrines were false, not that they were imposed by force—a form of persuasion long seen as normal."[12] The use of force as an acceptable way to gain control of the Middle East is another point to keep in mind in trying to understand the rapid expansion of Islam.

THE BIRTH OF ISLAM

According to Christopher Dawson, "The coming of Islam was the last act of a thousand years of interaction between East and West" and "Mohammed was the answer to the challenge of Alexander."[13] And according to Richard Bell, "The triumph of Islam in the East in the seventh century A.D. may be regarded as the judgement of history upon a degenerate Christianity."[14] Let us explore both observations. Before his death in 632, Muhammad created a sense of national unity among the warring tribes of Arabia. Treaties were made with Christian tribes, most of whom were Nestorian and Monophysite. In the treaty Muhammad himself made with the Christians of Najran, he granted them "protection for their religion and their churches and for monastic institutions, as well as for their bish-

The Expansion of Islam in the Early Years

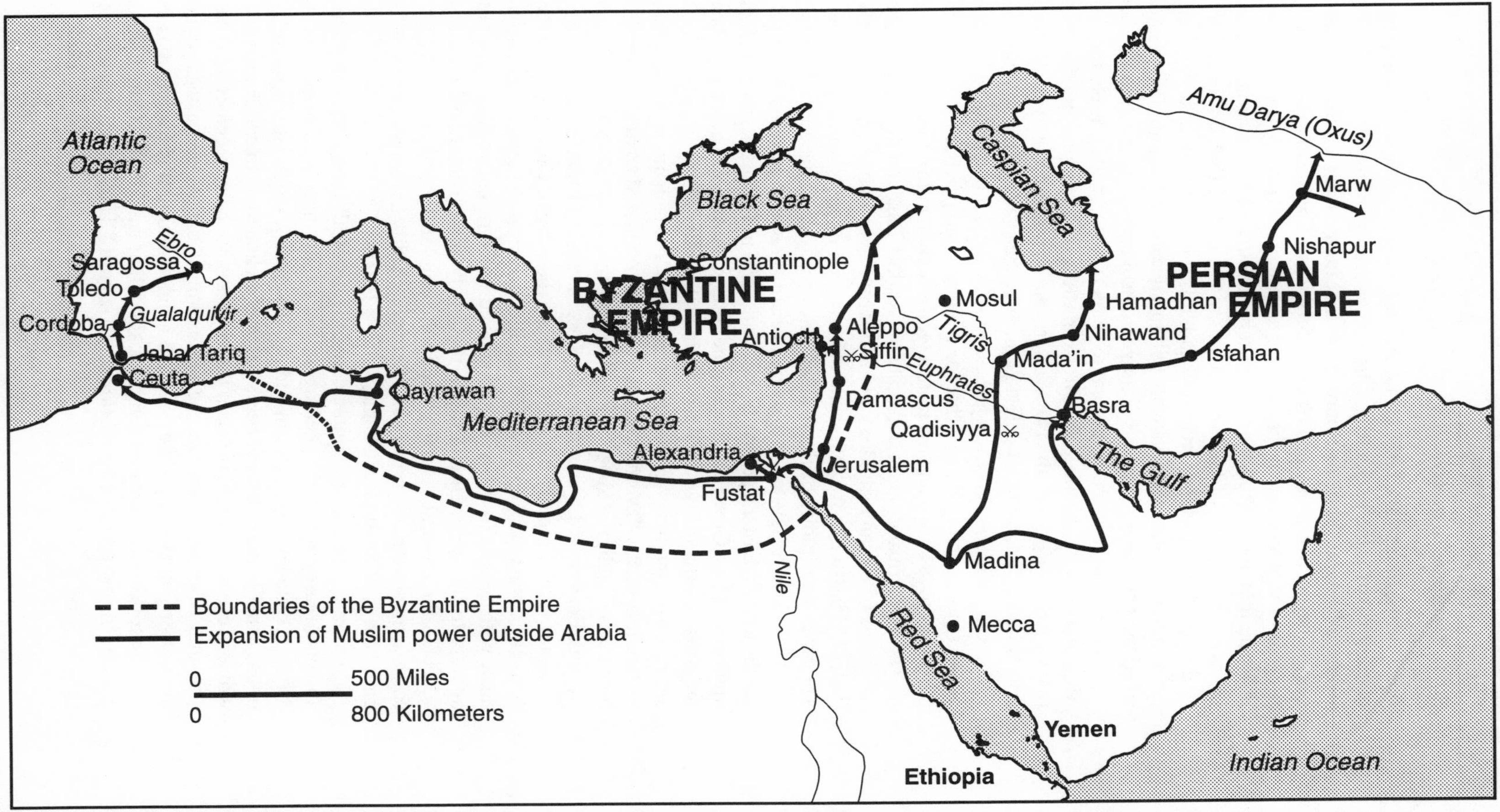
Atlantic Ocean
Ebro
Saragossa
Toledo
Cordoba
Gualalquivir
Jabal Tariq
Ceuta
Qayrawan
Mediterranean Sea
Alexandria
Fustat
Nile
Black Sea
Constantinople
BYZANTINE EMPIRE
Antioch
Aleppo
Siffin
Damascus
Jerusalem
Qadisiyya
Mosul
Tigris
Euphrates
Caspian Sea
Hamadhan
Nihawand
Mada'in
Basra
The Gulf
Madina
Mecca
Red Sea
Yemen
Ethiopia
Amu Darya (Oxus)
Marw
Nishapur
PERSIAN EMPIRE
Isfahan
Indian Ocean
Boundaries of the Byzantine Empire
Expansion of Muslim power outside Arabia
0
500 Miles
0
800 Kilometers

ops, priests, monks and hermits, none of whom were to be moved from his abode."[15] As for the pagan tribes, he succeeded in uniting them under the banner of Islam. While one may claim that many accepted the new faith only superficially, motivated by considerations of political expediency or the fear of violence rather than by any spiritual conversion, it is nonetheless true that many Arabs became true believers and jealous guardians of the primary sources of Islamic revelation: the text of the Qur'an and the traditions of what Muhammad said and did *(sunna)*. From these believers came statesmen and generals who, within a decade of Muhammad's death, freed the Middle East from Byzantine control and conquered the Persian Empire. From such believers came leaders who, within a century of Muhammad's death, made the Arabs masters of an empire greater than that of Rome at its zenith. The Western thrust into Europe was checked only when Charles Martel defeated them at the battle of the Pyrenees in 732. From such believers came jurists, mystics, and scholars who gave magnificent and undeniable proof that the doctrines and practices of Islam had the power to inspire many to create a glorious civilization and culture.

The Western attempt to dominate the Middle East and the use of force to spread Christian orthodoxy explain why it was into countries mainly under Christian control that Islam experienced its most rapid expansion. The amazing rapidity of the Arab advance was due to the cooperation of local Christians disgusted with Byzantine cruelty and oppression. Throughout the Middle East the people, being themselves not of Greek stock, looked upon everything Greek as a hateful and foreign intrusion. Therefore, when the Arabs came, many welcomed them as liberators from the hated Byzantine yoke, and many Christians even joined the Muslim army to defeat a common enemy.[16] Moreover, many in the conquered territories considered the new religion to be a kind of Arianism, a view held for a long time by both Eastern and Western theologians, including Luther.[17]

Islam spread rapidly not only because the official Christianity of the seventh century was oppressive, but also because of the way the Arabs dealt with people in the newly conquered territories. The Arabs did not attempt to impose their culture on the newly subjugated population but accepted the cultural diversity within the empire. For example, the Persians, who were neither Arabs nor Semites, readily accepted the new religion "but continued to speak and write in Persian."[18]

Moreover, the new religion cleared the air of all the inexplicable and abstruse reasoning of the theologians, since the notion of revelation is differently understood in Islam and in Christianity. In Christianity revelation is usually understood to be a system of right beliefs to which men and women respond in faith. In Islam the view is more comprehensive, in that although revelation contains the obligation of belief, it is a legal code through which God legislates over all human affairs. It is for this reason that the followers of the new religion called their way of life Islam, a word derived from the Arabic verb *aslama*, "to submit." They called themselves

Muslims, those who submit to God's law, from the active participle of *aslama*. The central concern of the Muslim is to obey the will of God, not to debate theological issues.

The emphasis on deed over creed is clear in the five pillars of Islam, four of which are things one should do, not ideas that one should believe. The first pillar, the profession of faith *(shahada)*, is a commitment to radical monotheism and to Muhammad as the instrument of God's will for humanity: "There is no god but God, and Muhammad is the Prophet of God." This profession marks the entrance into the Islamic community. The second pillar, prayer *(salat)* five times a day—daybreak, noon, midafternoon, sunset, and evening—is aimed at helping one keep in constant contact with God. The third pillar, almsgiving *(zakat)*, develops the link between religious practice and social concerns. The fourth pillar is fasting *(sawn)* during the month of Ramadan. Fasting schools one in compassion for the hungry and destitute and underscores one's human dependence on God. The fifth pillar is the *hajj*, the pilgrimage to Mecca, where Muslims believe that Abraham and Ishmael built the Ka'ba, the first temple to the one God. The five pillars combine a sense of personal responsibility, social awareness, and consciousness of belonging to the larger community of Islam.

Early Islam, in contrast to the official Christianity of the seventh century, was not rigid and closed. The interpretation of the law was a task for jurists. In the conquered territories they discussed the application of the law to contemporary problems in various parts of the empire, and out of these discussions developed numerous schools of law in different places such as Mecca, Medina, Damascus, Baghdad, and Kufa. Though the various schools accepted the Qur'an and the traditions of what Muhammad said and did *(sunna)* as infallible sources of revealed law, they interpreted the law to meet the social, cultural, and intellectual needs of diverse peoples through the use of analogical reasoning *(qiyas)*, that is, the application of the principles underlying a past decision to a new problem, and the principle of consensus of the local community *(ijma)*.

There was no one right interpretation of the law binding on all Muslims. In coping with diversity, the different schools respected each other's decisions, and differences of opinion among schools were regarded as a sign of God's mercy. Even today the Hanifite, Malikite, Shafi'ite, and Hanbalite schools of law divide the Islamic world among them. A Muslim is free to switch from one school to another, and different schools of law may even claim the allegiance of different members of the same family.[19]

The revealed law was entirely independent of secular authority because, as God's commands, it regulated the life of every Muslim, even a caliph's. That is to say, the early caliphs had no power to impose their preferred school of law on all Muslims. The distinction in the gospel of Mark between what is God's and what is Caesar's (Mk 12:17), which is fundamental to Christianity, has no parallel in classical Islamic thought. As Bernard Lewis explains,

[The caliph's] duty was not to expound, still less to interpret the faith, but to uphold and protect it, and to create and maintain conditions in which men could live the good Muslim life in this world, and thus prepare themselves for the world to come. To accomplish this, he had to preserve law and order within the frontiers of Islam against external attack. Where possible, it was his duty to extend those frontiers, until in the fullness of time the whole world was gained for Islam.[20]

Because Muslims consider their revelation to be a legal code through which God legislates over all human affairs, even the status of Christians with respect to Islam was determined by it. Muslim jurists divided the world into *dar al-Islam* (territory under Muslim rule) and *dar al-harb* (territory under non-Muslim rule), and the status of persons was determined by their religious affiliation. In territory under Muslim rule only Muslims enjoyed full citizenship. However, Islamic law recognized that Christians, Jews, Sabaeans, and Zoroastrians were "People of the Book," that is, people who had received a previous revelation from God, and so were entitled to the tolerance and protection of the Muslim state (Q 2:262; 5:69; 22:17). This principle of tolerance and protection was not extended to polytheists or idolaters. The fact that only Muslims were recognized as full citizens in the Islamic state is reminiscent of the fact that when Christianity became the official religion of the Roman Empire at the Council of Constantinople in 381, to be a citizen one had to be a Christian. In any event, the Islamic ideal was to fashion a world in which, under Muslim rule, idolatry and polytheism would be eliminated and "all people of the book could live in a society guided and protected by Muslim power."[21]

In keeping with the example of Muhammad in dealing with the Christians of Najran and the teaching of the Qur'an that "there is no compulsion in religion" (Q 2:256), Christians were permitted to remain in the territory of Islam through the making of treaties with the Muslim authorities. Many chose to do so rather than migrate to Christian lands where persecution in the name of orthodoxy was widespread. Those who were granted the status of permanent residents were called *dhimmis* and, under the terms of this status, had to agree to recognize the legality of their subjugation by paying a poll tax *(jizya)* and under some rulers accepting certain social restrictions with respect to the clothes they might wear, the beasts they might ride, the arms they might bear, and the like. They were also forbidden to proselytize the Muslims. In return the *dhimmis* obtained not only the protection of their lives and property, but also the right to practice their religion and to govern themselves by their own laws, enforceable by their own courts, in matters relating to the family, marriage, and inheritance.[22]

An example of such a treaty is the agreement between Caliph Umar I and the Christians living in Jerusalem when the city fell to the Arabs in 638. The treaty reads as follows:

The following are the terms of capitulation which I Umar, the servant of God, the Commander of the faithful, grant to the people of Jerusalem. I grant them security for their lives, their possessions, and their children, their Churches, their crosses and all that appertains to them in their integrity, and their lands, and to all their religion. Their Churches therein shall not be impoverished, nor destroyed, nor injured from among them; neither their endowments, nor their dignity and not a thing of their property; neither shall the inhabitants be exposed to violence in following their religion; nor shall one of them be injured.[23]

Moreover, the Arab rulers allowed Christian pilgrimages to Jerusalem after the conquest, and thousands of European Christians visited the Holy Land.[24]

Christians living permanently under Muslim rule were not forced to convert to Islam at the point of the sword.[25] In fact, in the late seventh century some Muslim leaders actually discouraged conversion because it reduced the poll tax and upset the budget.[26] Moreover, as we have already seen, Christians had actively participated in the conquests and in the first centuries Christians were in the majority in the Muslim state. Because they had a better education on the whole than the Arabs, they contributed greatly to the development of Islamic civilization. The civil administration of the empire was largely in their hands. They engaged in trade and commerce, rose to high positions in government, and generally shared in the vicissitudes of life of the Muslims. For example, the father of the Christian theologian John of Damascus was counsellor to the caliph 'Abd al-Malik (685-705), and John himself held a similar position till he withdrew to a life of seclusion in the monastery of Saba.[27]

Christians living in territory outside the jurisdiction of Islam were able to live as temporary residents in territory under Muslim rule if they were able to obtain a safe-conduct *(aman)*, which any Muslim of sound mind was free to grant. Temporary residents were called *musta'mins,* and the *aman* was ordinarily granted for a year. During this time Christians who were *musta'mins* were exempt from paying the poll tax and from many of the restrictions imposed on the *dhimmis*. However, if as temporary residents Christians overstayed their sojourn, the local Muslim authority had the right to deport them to their country of origin. Nonetheless, the common practice was to regard them as *dhimmis* and subject them to the obligations imposed on such persons.

The condition of Christians under Muslim rule should not be idealized, for they enjoyed only a protected status, and it is a fact that at certain times and places they suffered from discrimination and persecution.[28] For example, al-Hakim, the Fatimid ruler of Egypt (996-1020), did try to convert Christians by force. However, when he realized that his action was against Islamic law, he allowed his unwilling converts to return to Christianity. Again, when the Mongols invaded the heartland of Islam in the mid-thirteenth century, and some Christians rejoiced that Hulagu, under the influence of his Christian wife, persecuted the Muslims, the Muslims took their revenge after the Mongols were expelled. And in modern Turkey the movement for Greek independence combined with the religious sympathies it evoked in Europe did contribute to making the lot of the subject Christians harder than it would have been. Nevertheless, the very existence of so many Christian communities in countries under Islamic rule is "an abiding testimony to the toleration they have enjoyed, and shows that the persecutions they have from time to time been called upon to endure . . . have been excited by some local circumstances rather than inspired by a settled principle of intolerance."[29] Had the caliphs chosen to stamp out the Christian religion, "they might have swept away Christianity as easily as Ferdinand and Isabella drove Islam out of Spain."[30] Relationships between adherents of the two faiths were for the most part friendly, to the extent that they collaborated to create a civilization that was later to have a great impact on Western thought.

THE CRUSADES

The negative Islamic view of Christianity is due not only to the Middle East's experience of Byzantine Christianity, but also to its experience of Latin Christianity through the crusades. By way of background, it is helpful to recall that in the Great Schism of 1054 the Eastern (Greek) and Western (Latin) churches had separated over whether the Holy Spirit proceeds only from the Father, the Eastern formula, or whether the Holy Spirit proceeds both from the Father and the Son, the Western formula. It is helpful to recall also that in 1075 Pope Gregory VII, believing that the authority of the papacy ought to be as universal as the church it represented, had denied civil rulers the authority to make appointments to church offices. The conception of the supreme authority of the pope met with resistance from the emperor of Germany, Henry IV (1050-1106), who chose a counter pope, Guibert of Ravenna, who called himself Pope Clement III. After the death of Gregory VII in 1085, Urban II was elected pope in 1088. The result was that two popes contended for power to rule the world through the church of Rome. Clement resided in Rome and was supported by the imperial army. Urban II needed to make a bold move to secure the power of the papacy he so ardently desired.

An opportunity came in 1095 when the Byzantine emperor Alexius I (d. 1118) appealed to Urban II for help in dealing with the Turks. The Turks had crushed the Byzantines in the battle of Manzikert in 1071, and Alexius was faced with a resurgent Islam perilously close to Constantinople. It was this danger that prompted the Byzantine emperor to seek aid from the West. The appeal provided the opportunity that Urban so badly needed to gain recognition for papal authority and its right to legitimize temporal rulers. It was also an opportunity for him to try to reunite the Eastern and Western churches.

Recognizing that nothing unites like a common foe, Urban II summoned a council at Clermont in France and preached a holy war against the Muslims:

> Christian warriors, who seek without end for vain pretexts for war, rejoice, for you have today found true ones. You who have been so often the terror of your fellow citizens, go and fight against the barbarians, go and fight for the deliverance of the holy places; you who sell for vile pay the strength of your arms to the fury of others, armed with the sword of the Maccabees, go and merit an eternal reward. If you triumph over your enemies, the kingdoms of the East will be your heritage; if you are conquered, you will have the glory of dying in the very same place as Jesus Christ, and God will not forget that He shall have found you in His holy ranks. This is the moment . . . in which you may expiate so many violences *[sic]* committed in the bosom of peace. . . . If you must have blood, bathe your hands in the blood of the infidels. I speak to you with harshness, because my ministry obliges me to do so: so soldiers of hell, become soldiers of the living God! When Christ summons you to his defence . . . see nothing but the shame and the evils of the Christians: listen to nothing but the groans of Jerusalem.[31]

To rout the Muslims meant honor and booty for the feuding lords and barons of Western Europe. It meant the winning of political, economic, and military advantages in the Middle East. It meant an opportunity to gain indulgences that guaranteed the full remission of sins and the assurance of heaven. Understandably, the crowd responded with enthusiastic shouts of "God wills it!" Western Christianity had its jihad (holy war).

The first crusade was a pretext to justify Western intervention in the Muslim world. God may have willed it, "but there is certainly no evidence that the Christians of Jerusalem did, or that anything extraordinary was occurring there to prompt such a response at that moment in history."[32] The centuries of peaceful coexistence that had followed Umar I's treaty with the Christians of Jerusalem in 638 was shattered by holy wars. The crusaders captured Jerusalem in 1099. The Muslims reconquered it in 1187 under the leadership of Saladin (d. 1193). Subsequent crusades lasted well into the thirteenth century, until they degenerated into intra-Christian wars against those whom the papacy deemed to be heretics or schismatics.

Though the crusades, like the Byzantine oppression, left a trail of bitterness between Western Christians and Muslims that remains as a living factor in the world situation to the present day, they had little effect on the development of Muslim civilization. In this venture the Arabs, by a strange irony, became disciples of the very Greek learning that Alexander the Great had set out to spread in their lands a millennium before. At the time of the conquest of the Persian Empire many of the standard Greek works dealing with philosophy, medicine, astronomy, and the like had already been translated into Syriac. The first task the Arabs set themselves was to translate the Greek intellectual heritage from Greek and Syriac into Arabic. This translation project began before 800 but was properly organized by Caliph al-Ma'mun (813-33) in Baghdad. Nestorian and Monophysite Christians, as well as Jews, collaborated in translating the texts into Arabic. Muslims first studied Greek thought through these translations.[33]

Islamic learning was not restricted to the eastern region of the empire but was widely spread where Islam was strong. By the twelfth and thirteen centuries translators were at work in Spain and Sicily making translations from Arabic into Latin as Christian scholars tried to unearth the treasures of arabized Greek knowledge that had taken place in the ninth and tenth centuries in Baghdad. In Toledo, Archbishop Don Raimundo (1130-50) himself engaged in this undertaking. Thus the works of Aristotle, Euclid, Ptolemy, and other Greek writers were made available to the West. Avid scholars from every part of Europe rushed to Spain eager to acquire the riches of science and philosophy.[34]

The Muslims were not mere transmitters of Greek learning. They were the most advanced and daringly original thinkers of the time; "there was hardly a branch of learning, from logic and psychology to medicine, astronomy, and navigation, in which the influence of Moslem achievements was not readily discernible."[35] The scientific spirit then growing in Europe was stimulated by the Arabic stress on the importance of experiment.[36] "Christian scholasticism—even, indeed particularly, the masterful summation of St. Thomas Aquinas—would have been impossible without the philosophical texts and commentaries of Ibn-Sina, Al-Ghazzali, and Ibn Rushd, known to the West as Avicenna, Algazel, and Averroes."[37] So pervasive was the depth of Islamic thought that many scholars have seen its influence on the sublime imagery of Dante[38] and on the illustrious tradition of Spanish mysticism.[39]

In sum, the Muslim presence in Spain and Sicily from the eighth century onward and the European exposure to Muslim culture during the crusades had a significant influence on the development of Western thought. Because some Christian scholars have had a negative attitude toward Islam, they have tended to disparage the Muslim influence and exaggerated Europe's dependence on its Greek and Roman heritage. "So today an important task for . . . Western Europeans, as we move into the era of the one world, is to correct this false emphasis and to acknowledge fully [their] debt to the Arabic and Islamic world."[40]

THE OTTOMAN EMPIRE

The prestige of Islam passed from the Arabs to the Turks when they overthrew the Byzantine Empire with the capture of Constantinople in 1453, which, renamed Istanbul, became the capital of the Ottoman Empire. The Turks threatened the heart of Europe for almost two centuries. By the reign of Sulayman the Magnificent (1520-66) the Ottoman Empire was at the peak of its power. Its armies overpowered and subdued the Christian Balkan states, advanced across Hungary, and in 1529 laid siege to Vienna, the gateway to the West. The fate of Europe hung in the balance. This assault on Europe was frustrated, but efforts for its conquest lasted well into the seventeenth century when, in a second assault upon Vienna in 1683, John III of Poland inflicted a crushing defeat upon the Turkish forces. Incidentally, it was the pressure of the Turks on Vienna more than anything else that allowed the Reformation to flourish in Europe, for the forces of the Catholic princes, ever ready to give Protestantism the deathblow, had to be diverted to Vienna because of the danger of the Turkish invasion.[41]

The defeat of the Turks, coupled with the discovery of America and the sea route to India, lessened Europe's interest in the Middle East. Thus the great overland route through the Islamic world "was reduced to a trickle, and the cultural contacts between Christian Europe and the Islamic East also became of lesser importance."[42] The Islamic world remained a large self-sufficient bloc. "It did not need to trouble itself with Western Europe and the turmoil and unrest inside its borders."[43] Perhaps the Muslims even thanked God that the troublesome Europeans were now running wild into the wildernesses of America and leaving them alone. After all, they still held the center of the world stage—or so they thought.[44]

Whatever threat the Turks posed to Christians in Europe, as in the early Arab conquests, the Ottoman Empire's policy toward People of the Book living within its borders was magnanimous. Balkan peasants used to say, "Better the turban of the Turk than the tiara of the Pope."[45] Many Protestant scholars often contrasted Turkish tolerance with Catholic repression.[46] In sum, the Ottoman Empire was the classic example of a plural society. As Braude and Lewis note:

> Muslims, Christians and Jews worshipped and studied side by side, enriching their distinct cultures. The legal traditions and practices of each community, particularly in matters of personal status—that is, death, marriage, and inheritance—were respected and enforced through the empire.[47]

The peaceful isolation of the Ottoman Empire was soon shattered by developments in the West.

THE RISE OF COLONIALISM

By the eighteenth century Britain had lost its thirteen American colonies and the industrial age had started in Europe. The search for raw materials and markets saw the rise of colonialism. Europe literally burst its seams and had to expand. Clashes with the Islamic world began to occur once more as the land routes to Asia were opened up again in a new and growing commerce. All significant trade devolved into foreign hands, which resulted in the economic exploitation of the Middle East by Western powers.[48]

The situation worsened in the nineteenth century as Europe literally ingested the Islamic world bite by bite. "The great Moghol Empire which had ruled India was utterly defeated by the British." Malaya as well as Indonesia fell under European rule. "Egypt and the Sudan were dominated by foreigners, and North Africa and West Africa were subdued by the French." The Ottoman Empire, although stretching over vast expanses of land and still sovereign, was weak and labeled "the sick men of the Bosphoros." Persia was divided into British and Russian spheres of interest, "and all the northern tier of Islamic peoples was under Russian domination. Only the most inaccessible parts of the Islamic World, like Afghanistan, the Arabian inner deserts and the Yeman held out."[49]

With the coming of nineteenth-century colonialism, countries previously under Islamic rule were exposed to the influences of the West. The disruptive notions of European thought, the Enlightenment, liberalism, and nationalism, undermined the very different assumptions of Ottoman society. Moreover, modernity—in the eyes of Christian Europeans—was thought to be the result not simply of historical conditions that gave rise to the Enlightenment and the Industrial Revolution, but also of Christianity's inherent superiority as a religion and culture. For this reason the political challenge of colonialism was intensified by a wave of missionary activity that openly questioned the viability of Islam in the modern world. As Maxime Rodinson explains:

> The degraded state of the Muslim world made it an obvious target for Christian missionaries. The proselytizing crusade was launched with renewed vigor and quickly spread. . . . In keeping with the common beliefs of their time and normal inclinations, the missionaries credited the triumphs of European nations to Christianity while blaming the misfortunes of the Muslim world on Islam. The perception was that, if Christianity was inherently favorable to progress, then Islam must, by its nature, encourage cultural and developmental stagnation.[50]

Thus Christian missionaries often served the imperial aims of their home governments. The printing presses they founded helped disseminate the ideas of the West. In the schools and colleges they ran, the curriculum and language of instruction, even the teachers and textbooks, became largely French and English.

Scholarly opinion varies on the extent to which Christian missionaries collaborated with European powers in the domination of the Middle East. Perhaps Hugh Goddard's assessment of the issue is closer to the truth than that of Rodinson. According to Goddard:

> It can certainly be argued that circumstances varied very much from region to region and with respect to different European powers, but

on the whole what seems to have happened is that whereas in the early period of European expansion commercial and religious interests were pursued separately and even on occasion in opposition to each other, as the nineteenth . . . century progressed a greater measure of common interest and co-operation developed and there began to be more reference to "Christian civilization" on the part of both missionaries on the one hand and traders and political agents on the other.[51]

In any event, under colonialism the position of Christian minorities in the Ottoman Empire underwent a gradual but radical change. Initially they were *dhimmis*, People of the Book protected by Islam, with their rights and obligations set by Islamic tradition. But as the power of Europe increased, individual Christians were able to acquire a status resembling resident aliens, their rights and obligations fixed not by Islamic tradition but by foreign powers. Eventually Christian powers claimed the right to protect entire Christian communities in the empire. No longer people protected by Islam, Christian communities became people protected by Russia, France, and England. Tension ran high, for according to Islamic law it was not possible for them to be protégés of non-Muslim powers and be entitled to the protected status of *dhimmis* at the same time.[52]

To deal with the crisis the Ottoman government issued a number of edicts—the most important of which were the Gulhane Decrees of 1839 and the Hatti Himayun of 1856—that proclaimed the equality of all, Muslims and non-Muslims alike. Many among the Christian laity rejoiced at the removal of the social restrictions under which they lived. However, the hierarchy of the churches "consistently rejected the reforms fearing their power over their own millets [subjects] would be diminished."[53] "Muslims also rejected the reforms. For the Muslim Ottoman, Islam was the only true religion and thus he resented the government's effort at equalizing the status of the Dhimmis to that of himself."[54]

To the Turks it became increasingly clear that the Christian minorities constituted a potential danger to the Ottoman Empire from within. For them, Christian came to mean anti-Turkish and anti-national. Sporadic but violent persecutions followed. These persecutions—of Armenians, for example—"were religious in appearance, but in reality they were directed against groups no longer considered loyal to the state."[55] In the Christian West there was a great outcry, and the Turks were regarded as barbarians. This only served to strengthen the conviction of the Turks, and of Muslims in general, "that the Christian nations were united in a conspiracy against the world of Islam. To the Muslims it was not an issue of secularized power politics; it was an issue between Christianity and Islam."[56]

This conviction was not without some justification, for when the Muslim world reached its absolute low point after World War I, the Ottoman Empire fell apart and the heartland of the Arabs was occupied by Westerners. It found to its great consternation that it had no power to oppose its colonial masters. This vulnerability came as a rude awakening and a terrible shock because Muslims had come to equate their way of life with sovereignty. Suddenly, in their own realm, they found themselves ruled by a tiny minority of foreigners—Christians at that!—and there was nothing that they could do about it. At the Treaty of Versailles in 1919 Britain emerged as the supreme power in the Middle East, and King George V, de facto, became the ruler of more Muslims than any caliph in history.

THE RESURGENCE OF ISLAM

An extraordinary historical phenomenon had begun unfolding around 1800: the continuous, steady, and relentless occupation of Muslim lands by governments of Christian countries. Equally extraordinary was the way in which, responding to this long, drawn-out challenge, the Muslim world rolled Europe back. If in 1918 it was at its lowest point—humiliated, poor, exhausted and, almost at every point, subject to Christian domination—the end of the Second World War saw the collapse of colonialism. By the 1970s, as in the oil crisis, Islam stood before the world aggressive and with new confidence.

Muslims have discovered, however, that political colonialism has been replaced by economic colonialism. Victims of a past colonial subjugation, today they are still largely dependent on the economic, political, and social interests and systems dominated by Western free enterprise. This dependence is a form of neocolonialism, which Muslims feel they have to resist.

The resurgence of Islam has again raised concerns about the status and rights of Christians living in Muslim territory. It is true that most Muslim countries have granted Christians equality of citizenship, which legally entitles them to hold office in government. However, because of the revivalist mood in Islam today, and because of the past ties of Christians living in Muslim territory with colonialism and their continued association with the West, there are pressures from many quarters to exclude Christians from positions that formulate and implement the ideology of the state on the ground that the state's Islamic ideology requires a commitment to Islam.

Western critics of Islam see a restricted role for Christians living in an Islamic state as undemocratic and a denial of human rights. Muslim advocates of the move distinguish between Western and Islamic democracy by pointing out that the political ideology of the Islamic state is centered on the revealed law of God, not on human rights. For them Islam is not totalitarian or autocratic. The principle of consultation and consensus within the Muslim community *(ijma)* is proof of Islam's democratic spirit.[57]

In order to understand their position, it is helpful to recall that there is a difference between the Christian and Islamic conception of revelation.

Whereas for Christians revelation has the connotation of belief, for Muslims it has the character of law. Revelation for Muslims, as Rosenthal puts it, is

> not simply a direct communication between God and man, not only a transmission of right beliefs and convictions, a dialogue between a personal God of love, of justice and of mercy and man whom he has created in his image; it is also and above all a valid and binding code for man, who must live in society and be politically organized in a state in order to fulfil his destiny. In short, it is the law of the ideal state.[58]

Since Islam is a religion wedded to a political community that functions according to a law delivered to it by a prophetic lawgiver, the distinction between what is God's and what is Caesar's is not found in classical Islamic thought. In such a system there is no room for democratic parties based on human rights or for a non-Muslim competing religious worldview. All people should abide by the revealed law of Islam. If any individual or any group is in opposition, that person or group is in opposition to God's law.

It should be emphasized that before the rise of colonialism Christians living in Muslim countries enjoyed, on the whole, a measure of toleration the like of which cannot be found in Europe until quite modern times. It should be noted also, in the words of Charles Curran, that "Roman Catholic and mainline Protestant Christianity contributed little or nothing to the original acceptance of religious liberty in the West."[59] After the Reformation the Protestant churches met the challenge of religious diversity by claiming that the people should have the same religion as their prince. "Even when some churches gained religious liberty for themselves, as in England for example, they saw no need to extend it to others, such as Jews and Catholics."[60] The Protestant churches accepted religious liberty and human rights only after these ideas, advocated by the philosophers of the Enlightenment, were embodied in the French Revolution of 1789 and came to practical expression in the religious neutrality of civil government and civil law in many Western countries in the late eighteenth and early nineteenth centuries.

As for the Roman Catholic Church, it too was not at home with the separation of church and state. Its opposition to democracy and human rights gave birth to the famous claim that error has no rights. Catholic thinkers associated the Enlightenment idea of the "rights of man" with individualistic liberalism, which was opposed to the church's understanding of society "as an organic community of people working together for the common good."[61] For them, even "the language of rights indicated a human autonomy cut off from God and God's law."[62] In fact, the first unambiguous acceptance of religious liberty and human rights in official

Catholic teaching appeared only in 1963 with Pope John XXIII's encyclical *Pacem in Terris*.[63]

As we have seen, it took Christians a long time to work out the relationship of different faiths to democratic government. In the contemporary Islamic struggle with the issue we hear echoes of the same struggle in the Christian past. If today some Islamic states accept the dichotomy between religion and government, as in Turkey, it is not because of the teaching of Islam, but because of the impact of Western ideas on the Islamic world. Yet in resisting the West this much is clear: Muslims need Islam as they set about redressing the unfavorable balance of power in the world. If they were to weaken their attachment to Islam, they would undermine the very force that once made them great.[64]

If, prior to the rise of colonialism, the position of the non-Muslim under Muslim rule received much attention, the corresponding issue of the status of Muslims under non-Muslim rule hardly arose, and when it arose, it was discussed in the categories of permanent resident and temporary visitor. The position of the Muslim permanently resident in a non-Muslim land was considered in only one contingency, that of a person living in the non-Muslim world who converted to Islam. The majority of jurists insisted that such a person must migrate to a Muslim land and live under Islamic law. The question as to whether a Muslim can be a temporary resident in the non-Muslim world received more attention. Some Muslim jurists allowed it for the purpose of trade. Others allowed it if the person was able to obtain not only a safe-conduct *(aman)* but was also free to practice the Muslim religion for the duration of the stay.

When, under colonialism, the encounter with Europe brought large Muslim populations under non-Muslim rule, many jurists maintained that Muslims had an obligation to migrate to territory under Muslim rule. However, some Muslim jurists found authority in the principle of necessity *(darura)* in Islamic law for exemption from this obligation.

Today jurists have to make judgments about a new phenomenon— Muslims in search of permanent residence in the West. Though there have been a few such in the past, the voluntary migration of millions of ordinary Muslims to predominantly Christian countries has no precedent in history. The search for a solution to this phenomenon is only just beginning, both among Muslims and Christians.[65]

In this search theological input is central to finding an answer. If in the past theologians helped to alienate the two communities, today they have a duty to participate in the search for harmony. The following chapter will examine some of the theological issues involved in the contemporary Muslim-Christian encounter.

Questions for Discussion

1. What was the Christian response to religious and cultural diversity before the birth of Islam?

2. What was the Muslim response to the same issues after the birth of Islam?

3. How did the crusades contribute to the negative Islamic view of Christianity?

4. How did Islamic scholarship in the Middle Ages contribute to the development of Western thought?

5. What was the status of Christians living under Arab and Ottoman rule?

6. What role did colonialism play in undermining the Islamic world?

7. Account for the collapse of the Ottoman Empire by the end of World War I.

8. Explain the resurgence of Islam after World War II.

9. Compare the Muslim and Christian record on human rights.

10. What is the difference between the Christian and Muslim understanding of revelation, and how does this difference influence the Christian and Muslim understanding of human rights?

Suggested Readings

Arnold, T. W. *The Preaching of Islam.* New York: Scribner's, 1913.

Arnold, T. W., and Alfred Guillaume, eds. *The Legacy of Islam.* Oxford: Clarendon Press, 1931. Republished 1974.

Braude, Benjamin, and Bernard Lewis, eds. *Christians and Jews in the Ottoman Empire: The Functioning of a Plural Society.* New York: Holmes and Meier, 1982.

Esposito, John L. *Islam and Politics.* Syracuse, N.Y.: Syracuse University Press, 1984.

——————. *The Islamic Threat: Myth or Reality?* New York: Oxford University Press, 1992.

Kelly, Marjorie, ed. *Islam: The Religious and Political Life of a World Community.* New York: Praeger, 1984.

Kritzeck, James. *Sons of Abraham: Jews, Christians, and Moslems.* Baltimore and Dublin: Helicon, 1965.

Rouner, Leroy S., ed. *Human Rights and the World's Religions.* Notre Dame, Ind.: University of Notre Dame Press, 1988.

Schacht, J., and C. E. Bosworth, eds. *The Legacy of Islam.* Oxford: Oxford University Press, 1979.

Smith, Wilfred Cantwell. *Islam in Modern History.* Princeton: Princeton University Press, 1957.

Swidler, Leonard, ed. *Religious Liberty and Human Rights in Nations and Religions.* Philadelphia: Ecumenical Press, 1986.

Watt, W. Montgomery. *The Influence of Islam on Medieval Europe.* Edinburgh: Edinburgh University Press, 1972.

3

Theological Issues

THE NEGATIVE IMAGE OF ISLAM

Throughout the conflicts between the Christian West and the Muslim world, Europe in general remained largely ignorant of the religion of Islam. Because of secondhand reports full of misinformation—ignorance accentuated by unfamiliarity with Arabic—Christians had grossly mistaken views of Islam. At first, many Christians believed that Muhammad was an idol whom pagans worshiped as God. Others believed that he was a deliberate imposter who claimed to be the Messiah. Legends abounded to discredit the prophet and his revelation. According to one legend Muhammad suffered from "falling sickness" (epilepsy) and explained away his illness by saying that when the angel Gabriel appeared to him to deliver the message of the Qur'an, Gabriel was so dazzling that he was unable to stand thereafter.[1]

According to another legend in the West, Muhammad trained milk-white doves to sit on his shoulders to pick grain out of his ears and claimed that these doves came to him by the grace of the Holy Spirit to show that he was a prophet. There was also the story that Muhammad hung pots of milk and honey on a bull's horn to deceive the people by interpreting the milk and honey as symbols of the abundance that would come to them by merit of his works. Many believed that after his death by a sudden seizure on a dung hill, his body was eaten by swine. This legend provided an explanation for the Islamic prohibition against the eating of pork. No legend of the prophet was too extravagant. Many even scornfully declared that it is written in the Qur'an that two hundred and fifty ladies hanged themselves for the love of him. Of course, we know today that none of these legends is true.[2]

By the Middle Ages it was widely held in the West that Islam was a heretical form of Christianity. The conception of Christianity as the one universal religion carried with it the conviction that any religion that had arisen since the founding of Christianity must necessarily be nothing other than a treacherous offshoot from the true faith. In fact, it was widely held in the Middle Ages that Muhammad was a cardinal who failed to obtain election to the papacy "and who avenged himself by seceding from the Church and establishing a rival religion."[3]

Hence Dante (1265-1321) regarded him as a schismatic and doomed him to hell, where his fitting punishment was to be eternally chopped down the middle "from the chin to the fartwhole," spilling entrails and excrement at the door of Satan's stronghold.[4]

Dante's denigration of Muhammad in poetry is paralleled by what Aquinas did to him in theology. In his *Summa Contra Gentiles* (I,6,4) Aquinas claimed that "Muhammad forced others to become his followers by the violence of his arms." This is far from the truth. As we saw in the previous chapter, the choice between Islam and the sword was not imposed on Christians and Jews because they were People of the Book. It is also ironic that Aquinas should refer to Islam as a religion of violence, with the implication that Christianity is a religion of peace, when it was Christians who initiated the crusades that were in full force as Aquinas wrote.

In the same passage Aquinas also claimed that "no wise man, men trained in things divine and human, believed in [Muhammad] from the beginning. Those who believed in him were brutal men and desert wanderers." As we recall, Muslims not only became masters of the very Greek learning that Alexander had tried to impose on the people of the Middle East a millennium before, but were the most daring and advanced thinkers in the Middle Ages. In fact, it was Muslims who had introduced Aristotle to the West and eventually to Aquinas himself.

Western Christians were introduced to a more accurate understanding of Islam when a Latin translation of the Qur'an was prepared by Robert Ketton under the auspices of Peter the Venerable (1092-1156) in the middle of the twelfth century. Though the translation contained many errors and omissions, it launched a series of apologetic and polemical refutations of the Qur'an, including one by Peter himself. Martin Luther wrote an introduction to it when it was included in Theodore Bibliander's collection of translations from the Arabic, published in Basle in 1543, in order that Christians might know what an accursed and shameful book it was.[5] As for Muhammad, he was a false prophet; often he was portrayed as the anti-Christ, the beast of the Apocalypse, or the devil incarnate.

But knowledge of the Qur'an improved when Ludovico Marracci (1612-1700) published a faithful translation of it in 1698, even though his translation was accompanied by a long prologue refuting its errors. In 1705 Hadrian Reland of Utrecht published his *De Religione Mohammedica*, based on Muslim sources, but the book was placed "on the Roman Index because it seemed too favourable to Islam."[6]

About the same time, too, the first translations of the Qur'an appeared in European vernaculars. In 1649 Sieur du Ryer published his translation of the Qur'an into French, a work that was translated into English in the same year, with a caveat by Alexander Ross. Ross began his warning with these words:

> Good reader, the great Arabian imposter (Muhammad), now at last after a thousand years, is by way of France, arrived in England, and his Alcoran or Gallimaufrey of Errors (a Brat as deformed as the Parent, and as full of heresies as his scald Head was of scurf) hath learned to speak English.[7]

In these translations, as Samuel Chew points out, the "soaring eloquence which moves the Arabs to tears or to shouts of joy becomes in French, and still more in English, tasteless extravagance and bombast; the passages of homely wisdom and good counsel seem merely tedious platitudes, especially when this pedestrian version is set in contrast to the majestic language of the Authorized Version of the Bible." Chew goes on to say that the same strictures apply in large measure to the translation of George Sale (1734), which in the eighteenth century superseded this; for despite the great learning of Sale, "his version fixed in the English mind the notion that the Qur'an is a stupid, verbose and extravagant book."[8]

Nevertheless, the eighteenth century brought with it a clearer understanding of the Qur'an, because the new age of the Enlightenment saw a deep kinship to its own spirit in the rigorous monotheism of Islam, in its strong moral emphasis, and in the loving devotion of its mystics.

IRENIC VOICES

Parallel to polemical writers were evangelistic efforts. Almost the first Christian attempt to use a missionary method to convert the Muslims was that of St. Francis of Assisi (1182-1226) at the beginning of the thirteenth century. He was convinced that if Muslims were not converted, it was because the gospel had not been presented to them in its simplicity and beauty. At the height of the crusades Francis visited the Sultan of Egypt and then returned to Italy, where he wrote the famous "Canticle of All Creatures" in phrases reminiscent of the Qur'an. Impressed by the Muslim call to prayer, he encouraged the friars to have church bells announce the Christian services. It would appear that Francis was more impressed by the Muslims than they were by him.

Associated with the Franciscans was the layman Raymond Lull (1235-1315), a Catalan philosopher, poet, and missionary. According to Annemarie Schimmel:

> His great novel, *Blanquerna*, best expresses his attitude to and understanding of Islam. Here, as in other early works, . . . he praises

the Muslims' faith in the unity of God, which he views as the basis on which the three "Abrahamic" religions could understand one another: he acknowledges the importance of the Sufi practice of *dhikr* ("recollection of God") and describes it as a useful step on the way to God; finally, he expresses the opinion that Muslims are closer to Christians than are other nonbelievers because they accept the virgin birth of Mary.[9]

Then there were the writings of the Dominican scholar-missionaries William of Tripoli (1220-73) and Ricoldo de Monte Crucis (1243-1320), written at the end of the thirteenth century. Unlike Peter the Venerable and other Western scholars who knew no Arabic, they knew the language and wrote after prolonged acquaintance with the Islamic scripture and traditions, and after many years experience of how Islam works in the actual life and conduct of its adherents. In his *On the Condition of the Saracens*, William of Tripoli gave a penetrating analysis of those points on which Islam and Christianity are more or less in agreement. He did not present Muhammad as a criminal imposter but dwelt upon the praise the Qur'an gives to God's power, mercy, and justice. He also noted the high honor it gives to the Old Testament prophets and, above all, to Jesus. "His conclusion was that Islam has its share of right and truth and the Moslem is not far from Christian belief."[10]

Ricoldo de Monte Crucis in his *Confutatio Alcorani* also acknowledged the virtues of Islam. He pointed out to his fellow Christians that in many respects Muslims can offer examples worthy of imitation. He praised the Muslims for their hospitality, their zeal for study, their charity to the poor, their spirit of unity, their respect for Jesus and the prophets, their devotion to prayer, and their reverence for God.[11]

Again, after the fall of Constantinople to the Ottomans in 1453, George of Trebizond (1395-1484)[12] and John of Segovia[13] (1400-58) actively campaigned for a Christian-Muslim peace conference, while Nicholas of Cusa[14] (1401-1464) explored the idea of the ultimate unity of all religions. Nicholas's tolerance for religious diversity emerges in his *De Pace Fidei* (1453-54), while his *Cribratio Alcoran* (1461) "is perhaps the most tolerant examination of Islam in the late medieval West."[15]

Even Alexander Ross, who wrote two hundred years later, and who considered Islam to be heretical, had a very high opinion of Muslims. In the very caveat to his translation of the Qur'an he wrote: "If we observe their Justice, Temperance, and other moral virtues, we blush at our own coldness, both in devotion and charity . . . ; and surely their devotion, piety, and works of mercy are the main causes of the growth of Mahometism."[16]

The virtues of Islam continued to impress outsiders through the centuries. For example, in the nineteenth century Charles de Foucauld (1858-1916)[17]—who as a boy even the Jesuits found unteachable, and who as a young man defied the French army because of a romantic relationship—

came to understand, when exposed in Morocco and Algeria to the virtues of Islam, that there is something greater and more real than the pleasures of the world. De Foucauld's conversion to faith through his encounter with Muslims is one of Islam's gifts to Christianity, not only because of the sanctity of his life, but also because of the inspiration he provided for the foundation of the Little Brothers and Sisters of Jesus.

Though by the end of the nineteenth century many scholars and missionaries had come to recognize certain Islamic values, none went so far as to recognize the legitimacy of Islam after Christianity, of Muhammad after Jesus, or of the Qur'an after the gospels. And so, in the twentieth century controversy and refutation were still fundamental elements in Muslim-Christian relations, but discovery and recognition of Islam's authentic values gradually gained ground.

Miguel Asin y Palacios (1871-1944), a Spanish Catholic priest, from his study of Muslim-Christian similarities in the field of philosophy and mystical theology, was the first to show how Islam and Christianity are unavoidably linked together in the religious history of humankind. Never before had a Christian in full loyalty to his own religious tradition been so aware of this.

However, the scholar who contributed the most to the modern Christian reappraisal of Islam was Father Louis Massignon (1883-1962). Like de Foucauld, Massignon rediscovered his Catholic faith through his encounter with Islam. He was convinced that Abraham was the forefather of Judaism, Christianity, and Islam, and he[18] and his supporters[19] accepted the connection of Muslims to Abraham through Ishmael.

THE STORY OF ABRAHAM

Let us have a closer look at the story of Abraham because of its importance for the contemporary Muslim-Christian dialogue. According to the book of Genesis, when God called Abraham to migrate from Chaldea, God made him a promise that he would be the father of a great nation (Gn 12:1-3) and that his descendants would be as many as the stars in the sky (Gn 15:1-6). When Abraham left home, however, his wife Sarah was barren (Gn 11:30). As years rolled by and Sarah had no child, she conceived the idea that Abraham should assist the divine promise with a little help from her maid. So she brought her maid Hagar to him, and Hagar became pregnant. Then Sarah became jealous of Hagar and persuaded Abraham to banish the poor woman into the desert. However, the angel of the Lord appeared to Hagar by a spring of water and told her that she would have a son whom she was to call Ishmael, and that God would "greatly multiply your offspring that they cannot be counted for multitude" (Gn 16:10).

After Ishmael was born, Sarah became pregnant and gave birth to Isaac (Gn 17:19). When Abraham was told of the birth of Isaac, he nevertheless interceded with God on behalf of his son Ishmael (Gn 17:18). God heard his prayer and said, "As for Ishmael, I have heard you; I will bless him and make him fruitful and exceedingly numerous; he shall be the father of twelve princes, and I will make him a great nation" (Gn 17:20). And when Hagar and her son were dying of thirst in the wilderness, the angel of the Lord showed her a spring and saved them (Gn 21:15-21). The threatened life of Ishmael was thus safeguarded by divine intervention. God's rescue of Ishmael in the wilderness parallels the rescue of Isaac from the sacrifice in the land of Moriah (Gn 22:1-14). And while it is true that God made his eternal covenant with Isaac and not with Ishmael (Gn 17:19-21; cf. 21:12-13), it is nonetheless true that Ishmael was accepted into God's covenant with Abraham thirteen years before Isaac was born, when Abraham circumcised himself and Ishmael, strikingly on the same day (Gn 17:10-11, 23-26). Genesis gives a list of Ishmael's descendants, naming the twelve princes descended from him who unmistakably point to Arabia (Gn 25:13-15).

Through Isaac and Ishmael we have two parallel lines of Abraham's descendants. The line of Abraham and Isaac leads to Jerusalem and to Jesus. The line of Abraham and Ishmael leads to Mecca and Muhammad. The two parallel lines of Abraham's descendants endow Arabia and the Arabs with an honored place in monotheist history—one genealogically independent of Jews and Christians.

In the story of Abraham it is relevant to emphasize that Abraham was neither a Jew, nor a Christian, nor a Muslim. Yet the members of these three religions regard him as their spiritual ancestor. In so doing, they acknowledge that there is a true knowledge of the one God apart from that found in their own understanding of monotheism. Abraham was aware of this simple yet profound truth, for in his own lifetime there was already a monotheistic presence in Jerusalem under the leadership of Melchizedek (Gn 14:18-20). Yet Abraham received a blessing from Melchizedek. His acceptance of Melchizedek's blessing shows his understanding that worship of the one supreme God can take different forms.[20]

In Abraham's choice of the cave Makhpelah as his burial place, he again affirmed that monotheism can have more than one expression, for *Makhpelah* in Hebrew means "multiplicity." To accentuate the point that religious pluralism can exist on a common monotheistic foundation, the Genesis story tells us that Ishmael returned from the desert when Abraham died. In spite of their previous separation Ishmael and Isaac, in an act charged with symbolism, buried their father in the holy cave (Gn 25:9). The fact that Ishmael is not cast away has theological significance for Christian-Muslim relations, as we shall see.

In the Qur'anic version of the story of Abraham there is no mention of Hagar or Sarah, nor is there any suggestion that Ishmael was rejected in favor of Isaac. In fact, Ishmael remains closely related to his father, and in so doing remains firmly within the Abrahamic monotheistic tradition. Of him we read in the Qur'an:

> And make mention in the Scripture of Ishmael. Lo! He was a keeper of his promise, and he was a messenger (of Allah), a Prophet; he enjoined upon his people worship and almsgiving, and was acceptable in the sight of the Lord (Q 19:54-55).

The Qur'an states explicitly that Abraham together with Ishmael rebuilt the Ka'ba at Mecca, where they both prayed that God would make their descendants a great nation to whom God would send a messenger who would recite God's revelation (Q 2:125-29; 22:26-29). Muslims see the answer to this prayer in the Prophet Muhammad.

From the time of John of Damascus (d. ca.750) Christian polemicists against Islam accepted the Arab's Abrahamic descent but interpreted it in a wholly negative manner. Influenced by a passage in Paul's letter to the Galatians, they called Muslims Ishmaelites or Hagarenes with the object of excluding them from the covenant and the legacy of Abraham.[21] The passage on which their interpretation was based reads as follows:

> Tell me, you who desire to be subject to the law, will you not listen to the law? For it is written that Abraham had two sons, one by a slave woman and the other by a free woman. One, the child of the slave, was born according to the flesh; the other, the child of the free woman, was born through the promise. Now this is an allegory: these two women are two covenants. One woman, in fact, is Hagar, from Mount Sinai, bearing children for slavery. Now Hagar is Mount Sinai in Arabia and corresponds to the present Jerusalem, for she is in slavery with her children. But the other woman corresponds to the Jerusalem above: she is free, and she is our mother (Gal 4:21-26).

Today scholars point out that Paul could not have intended to exclude Muslims from the covenant in this passage, since Islam came into being many centuries after his death. They claim that the children of Hagar in the passage referred to Jewish Christians who maintained that the true children of Abraham are those who believe in Christ but also keep the law given in the Torah, a view with which Paul vehemently disagreed.[22] For Paul, the true children of Abraham are those who are his children by faith alone. As he says in the same letter to the Galatians, Abraham "believed God, and it was reckoned to him as righteousness" (Gal 3:6), and anyone who, like Abraham, unconditionally puts his trust in God is a child of Abraham (Gal 3:7; also Rom 4:16).

Additionally, for the Qur'an, as for Paul, it is faith, not physical descent, that makes us children of Abraham. Physical descent from Abraham is of no use for salvation if faith is lacking (Q 2:124). For the Qur'an (Q 16:120-23), for Paul (Rom 4:18), and even for the letter to the Hebrews (11:8-12), Abraham is the primal model of faith for all human beings because it was in faith alone, despite many trials, that he was found to be loyal and obedient to God.

Since faith, not physical descent, is the fundamental criterion for determining who are children of Abraham both in Muslim and Christian perspective, the denial by some scholars[23] that Ishmael is the ancestor of the Arabs should not keep Christians from affirming the Abrahamic status of Islam. For Christians claim that they are children of Abraham by being his spiritual heirs, not by being his physical descendants.

The Qur'an claims, however, that Muslims are closest in faith in Abraham (Q 3:68) since Jews and Christians were constantly disputing with each other (Q 23:53; 2:113) and Christians had succumbed to dogmatic disputes among themselves. It is important to recognize here that in spite of the Qur'anic claim, nowhere does the Qur'an say that Muslims are exclusively the children of Abraham. More concretely, while the Qur'an maintains that Abraham was neither a Jew nor a Christian, since the Torah and the gospel came long after him (Q 3:65-67), nowhere does it deny that Jews and Christians are children of Abraham.[24]

Although Louis Massignon (1883-1962), the scholar who contributed the most to the modern Christian reappraisal of Islam, was swimming against the tide of Catholic opinion in championing the idea that Islam is an Abrahamic religion, there is support for his position in a papal document written almost one thousand years ago, and then forgotten.

In 1076 the Muslim ruler al-Nasir of Bijaya, now in modern Algeria, wrote to Pope Gregory VII requesting that a local priest, Severandus, be ordained bishop to care for Christians in his domain. In reply the pope, among other things, said, "You and we owe this charity to ourselves especially because we believe in and confess one God, admittedly in a different way, and daily praise and venerate him." The pope concluded the letter with wishes for al-Nasir's health and a prayer that "after the long space of this life that same God will lead you into the bosom of blessedness of the most holy patriarch Abraham."[25] The pope's prayer acknowledges that a Muslim is a child of Abraham, and the tenor of the letter implies that Christians and Muslims form a family in faith through a common ancestor. Neal Robinson has observed that this letter, written "some twenty years before the First Crusade, suggests that had it not been for Urban II's ill-fated decision, Christian-Muslim relations might have developed somewhat differently."[26]

RETHINKING REVELATION

While Massignon was hard at work helping Christians to reevaluate their estimate of Islam, the end of the Second World War and the collapse of colonialism saw many non-Christian countries win their independence from Europe. Perhaps because Christianity was closely allied to colonialism, theologians took the opportunity to reflect on the legitimacy of the world religions generally. Many of them, notably the German Jesuit Karl Rahner,[27] began to see that history as a whole was the general history of salvation. In defending this view they made a distinction between general and special revelation.

It is helpful to recall here that for centuries most Catholic theologians understood Christian revelation to be truths disclosed by God that are indispensable for our salvation. Moreover, the idea that revelation ended with the last apostle and was stored in a "deposit of faith" rendered revelation something static, past and closed. Correlative to this cognitive approach to revelation with its accent on propositional truths was the understanding of faith as primarily belief. This "truths-beliefs" paradigm led many Christians to believe that if they acknowledge the propositions to be true on the authority of God mediated through the church, they will enter the salvation promised to them. For them, non-Christian revelations before Christ were a preparation for the gospel. These revelations were abrogated with the coming of Christ. In this view the Qur'an, coming after Christ, cannot be a revelation from God.

In contrast to this understanding of revelation Rahner insisted that revelation is fundamentally the self-communication of God to the world, not just the Judeo-Christian world. For him, revelation has a general character that is broader than the special revelation that God disclosed in the person of Christ.

Building on Rahner's thinking theologians[28] have emphasized the interpersonal character of revelation and have applied to it the basic metaphor of personal encounter. In keeping with this metaphor they say that revelation cannot be reduced to information from the "Beyond" but must include the human response to the self-communication of God. They emphasize that the human response is always historically contextualized in accord with the given potential of linguistic expression, a potential always defined by the given social, political, cultural, and religious circumstances of those to whom the communication is addressed. Since revelation occurs and is expressed within a given historical situation, community, and tradition, there is a Jewish revelation, a Christian revelation, an Islamic revelation, and so on.[29]

In Paul's words, revelation is a treasure we possess "in clay jars, so that it may be made clear that this extraordinary power belongs to God and does not come from us" (2 Cor 4:7). Put differently, God and human beings are the co-authors of revelation. As Jacques Dupuis explains, "Because God is the author, it is not reducible to a human pronouncement concerning God. But because the human being is the author as well, this word addressed by God to human beings is authentically a human word—the only word, after all, that would be intelligible to them." He goes on to say that in affirming that the Bible is the word of God in human words, Christian theologians make use of the concept of inspiration, by which they mean "that God, while respecting the human author's activity, guides and assumes this activity in such wise that what is written is, in its entirety, the word of God to the human being."[30]

The concept of inspiration acknowledges that the word of God expressed in human words "does not suppress, in those who transmit the revelation, the limitations nor the imperfections that are the lot of the human condition." There is no divine scripture in the pure state, "but there are expressions of the word of God across modes of speech and action specifically human."[31] In the contemporary theology of revelation the limitation of every human and cultural expression of the word of God can explain, at least in part, the divergences between revelations. "It is not God who is self-contradictory, but those who speak in God's name."[32]

In the context of what has just been said, it is important for Christians to be aware that according to the Christian faith the fullness of revelation is not the written word of the New Testament but the person of Jesus Christ. The New Testament is the human record, the authentic memoir of the self-communication of God in Christ. The New Testament itself admits that it reports the fullness of revelation through Christ only incompletely (Jn 20:30; 21:25). In any case, this is the understanding of *Dei Verbum*, the Vatican II document on revelation, when it distinguishes the fullness of revelation in the person of Jesus (no. 4) from its transmission in the New Testament (no. 7).

The understanding of revelation as personal encounter with God does not lead to relativism or indifference, since the quality of a person's faith is not measured by the exactness of its formulation. Across the human expressions of the revelation of God the faith of an authentic believer truly reaches the fullness of divinity. Thomas Aquinas put it well when he wrote, "The act of faith does not end with the formula [of church or our personal ideas], but at the very reality of God."[33]

In sum, general revelation is the means by which God has communicated and continues to communicate with humanity. The world religions are the setting for this general revelation, and, as a consequence, people can be saved by a grace expressed in terms of their own revelation. That is, the world religions are the extraordinary ways of salvation for the majority of humanity, and the message of their founders is revelation from God in a real sense, although incomplete. The Judeo-Christian revelation is the special revelation or history represented by Israel or Christianity, which offers the ordinary way of salvation. This distinction between general and special revelation recognizes the legitimacy of the world religions, and so of Islam, as positively desired by God in the general history of salvation.

The recognition that the human response to the self-communication of God, general or special, is always conditioned by history and culture shifts the understanding of revelation from one that is absolute, static, and exclusive to one that is dynamic and relational. This shift makes interreligious dialogue not only possible but even necessary in today's world. It can enable people with different revelations to learn how others perceive their own views, to perceive views other than their own as a source of knowledge and insight, to adapt elements from other revelations that they find enriching, to face the challenge of new questions generated by dialogue, to work for social justice for all, and to focus on building a consensus on a global ethic as we face the problems of the twenty-first century.[34]

ISLAM AND RELIGIONS OF THE BOOK

The Islamic distinction between inspiration and revelation complements the distinction contemporary Christian thinkers make between general and special revelation. For Muslim thinkers, general revelation is the guidance that God communicates to all through inspiration; this guidance can be received through objective reflection on nature (Q 2:164; 3:190; 30:23-25) as well as through logic and inference, as in the study of history (Q 20:128). Special revelation (*wahy*) is the communication that God gave to prophets up to Muhammad, "the seal of the Prophets" (Q 33:40).[35]

According to Fazlur Rahman,[36] though Muslims regard the Qur'an as the final special revelation from God, they believe that each previous special revelation contains the same basic message that there is only one God. Moreover, they believe that though each prophet received his message in his own language (Q 16:36), all the messages came from a single source, an eternal book in heaven called the "Mother of the Book" (Q 43:4; 13:39) and the "Hidden Book" (Q 56:78). It is for this reason that Muhammad declares in the Qur'an that he believes not only in the Torah and the gospel but "in whatever Book God may have revealed" (Q 42:15). This follows from the fact that God's guidance is universal and not restricted to any one people: "And there is no nation wherein a warner has not come" (Q 35:24) and "for every people a guide has been provided" (Q 13:7).

It is important to note that the Qur'an makes no exclusivist claim that the acceptance of its revelation is necessary for salvation. Even when replying to the Jewish and Christian claims that salvation comes only through acceptance of their particular revelation (Q 2:113; 2:111; 3:120), the Qur'an says: "Whoever surrenders himself to God while he does good deeds as well, he shall find his reward with his Lord, shall have no fear, nor shall he come to grief" (Q 2:112). Elsewhere the Qur'an explicitly acknowledges that Jews and Christians are saved through their own revelation: "Surely those who believe [that is, Muslims] and those who are Jews, and Christians, and Sabaeans—whoever believes in God and the Last Day and does what is right—shall be rewarded by their Lord: they have nothing to fear or to regret" (Q 2:62).

In holding that all prophetic messages came from a single source, Muslims understand the multiplicity of expression of God's basic message that there is only one God to be the result of the culture, history, and language that corresponds to the time and place in which each revelation was received. Thus for the Muslim scholar Mahmoud Ayoub,[37] as for many contemporary Christian thinkers, divergent expressions of revelation are willed by God. Moreover, Mohamed Talbi points out that the Qur'an itself states:

> And We have sent down to you the Book in truth confirming the Book that existed already before it. . . . For each one of you [several communities] We have appointed a Law and a way of Conduct [while the essence of religion is identical]. If God had so willed, He would have made you all one community, but [He has not done so] that He may test you in what He has given you; so compete in goodness. To God shall you all return and He will tell you [the Truth] about what you have been disputing (Q 5:48).[38]

No human expression of God's word can claim to exhaust the mystery of God or to represent the entirety of the word of God. Just as for Christians the fullness of revelation in Christ transcends any expression of it in human words, as in the New Testament, so too for Muslims the fullness of revelation contained in the "Mother of the Book" transcends any expression of it, as in the Qur'an, for the Qur'an itself declares: "Were the oceans to be ink for the words of my Lord, the oceans would be exhausted, even if we were to bring many oceans like it without end" (Q 18:110).

Since divergent expressions of revelation are willed by God, the Qur'an, as all written revelations, is both the word of God and a human book. As Mahmoud Ayoub explains,[39] according to Muslim tradition it is the word of God, for when Muhammad heard this word, it sounded as a reverberating bell. It is also the word of God because Muhammad had the experience of seeing the angel Gabriel, who dictated the revelation (Q 2:97). For Muslims the audition and vision testify to an invasive power that took control of Muhammad's human senses. It was with the suspension of his senses, Muslims believe, that Muhammad received the words dictated to him by the angel. The Qur'an is the record of those words; thus it reproduces the word of God.

As we recall, Muslims distinguish between inspiration and revelation. For them, inspiration is the general guidance that God communicates to all reflective persons. Special revelation is the communication that God gave to prophets. Thus the Qur'an is not an inspired text in the sense in which Christians understand the Bible to be an inspired text, where God guided the activity of the human author so that what was written is the word of God. Because the Qur'an records the words dictated to Muhammad by the angel Gabriel, the dictation is divine rather than human speech (Q 9:6); it has a significance for Muslims similar to that of the Logos in Christianity. Worthy of note here is the fact that the only miracle that the Qur'an admits to is that of the Qur'an itself, an inimitable scripture in perfect Arabic that no human being, least of all an unlettered person, as Muhammad was (Q 7:157), could emulate (Q 2:23-24).

While the Qur'an is the word of God, it is also a human book, for when it was communicated to Muhammad, it was not dictated to him from the "Hidden Book" in heaven in its original form, but in an Arabic version intelligible to him and his people. As the Qur'an itself admits: "Had We revealed the Qur'an in a foreign tongue they would have said: 'If only its verses were expounded! Why in a foreign tongue, when the Prophet is Arabian?'" (Q 41:44). Paradoxically, though the Qur'an was revealed, not inspired, it is nonetheless the word of God in human words.

Mahmoud Ayoub further observes that while the Qur'an is the word of God it is "also an earthly book whose history is intimately tied to the life and history of an earthly community,"[40] shaping it and being shaped by it. In support of his view he points out that "many verses were revealed in answer to a particular problem in the life of the community. Thus *asbab al-nuzul* or 'occasions of revelation' have bound the Qur'an to human history."[41] He concludes his observation by saying "that the Qur'an shares in our humanity in entering fully into history in the same way that Christ the eternal Logos entered into our humanity as well."[42]

Thus there is a human dimension to God's revelation in both Christianity and Islam. The essential difference is that for Christians the word of God is a person, while for Muslims it is a book. In this, as Fazlur Rahman observes: "The Qur'an would most probably have no objection to the Logos having become flesh if the Logos were not simply identified with God and the identification were understood less literally. For the Qur'an, the word of God is never simply identified with God."[43] In any case, just as Christians are nourished by their word of God through the eucharist, so Muslims are nourished by their word of God through the interiorization of the Qur'an in prayer.

In sum, the special revelation of the Qur'an recognizes that Christians and Muslims have been recipients of the message that there is only one God: "You will find the nearest of all people in friendship to the Believers [that is, Muslims] those who say they are Christians" (Q 5:82). Based on this fraternal attitude which has no parallel to other religious communities, the Qur'an even issues an invitation to Christians to come together for dialogue to form common cause under one God: "O People of the Book! Let us come together upon a formula which is common between us—that we shall not serve anyone but God" (Q 3:64). The contemporary Muslim-Christian dialogue is in search of such a formula.

VATICAN II AND WORLD RELIGIONS

Vatican II was greatly influenced by contemporary thinking on revelation. When the council addressed the question of religious pluralism, *Dei Verbum*, its document on revelation, was more attuned to salvation history, more personalistic and less propositional than previous Catholic documents on the subject. Revelation was no longer understood as statements about God from God. Such doctrinal formulations were seen as secondary to the more fundamental recognition that revelation is a human response to the self-communication of God.

Lumen Gentium, the council's document on the constitution of the church, abandoned the church's previous negative attitude to non-Christian religions and made it official that all religions can be instruments of salvation (no. 16)—a view in keeping with theologians like Rahner, studying non-Christian religions. *Ad Gentes*, the decree on the church's missionary activity, affirmed that there is truth and grace among the nations "as a sort of secret presence of God" (no. 9). The decree goes on to say that Christians can "learn by sincere and patient dialogue what treasures a bountiful God has distributed among the nations of the world" (no. 11). Thus the good found in non-Christian religions is not reducible to subjective dispositions of the human heart but extends to objective elements in the religious traditions themselves.

Moreover, *Nostra Aetate*, the declaration on the relationship of the church to non-Christian religions, in speaking of all non-Christian religions, explicitly stated that the church "rejects nothing which is true and holy in these religions, that in fact she looks with sincere respect upon their ways of conduct, life and teachings which, while differing in many respects from what she holds, nevertheless often reflect the brightness of that Truth which enlightens" men and women everywhere (no. 2). Furthermore, *Nostra Aetate* exhorted Catholics "through dialogue and collaboration with the followers of other religions, and in witness of Christian faith and life, to acknowledge, preserve and promote the spiritual and moral goods found among them as well as the values found in their society and culture" (no. 2). Through statements such as these the church has acknowledged that she does not have a monopoly on the Holy Spirit.

Following the lead of Vatican II, Pope John Paul II, in his encyclical *Redemptor Hominis*, affirmed that religion is a universal phenomenon linked with humankind's history and consequently that we should impose no strict limits in its exploration. He speaks glowingly of the "magnificent heritage of the human spirit that has been manifested in all religions" (no. 12). He says that the many religions witness "to the primacy of the spiritual . . . with direct effects on the whole of culture" (no. 11) and goes on to say that they are the "many reflections of the truth, 'seeds of the Word,' attesting that though the routes taken may be different, there is but a single goal . . . a quest for God and . . . for the full meaning of human life" (no. 11).

For John Paul II, openness to other religions is not a betrayal of commitment but often a call to faith, as when he says that "the firm belief of the followers of non-Christian religions—a belief that is also an effect of the Spirit operating outside the visible confines of the Mystical Body—can make Christians ashamed at being often themselves so disposed to doubt concerning the truths revealed by God" (no. 6).

In acknowledging that the Spirit acts outside the visible confines of the church, John Paul II rejects past references to non-Christians as heathens, pagans, or enemies of God. While upholding that Christians must witness to the special revelation of God in Christ, he calls on them to respect "all that the Spirit, who 'blows where it wills' (see John 3:8), has done in members of other religious faiths" (no. 12) through general revelation. Moreover, because he recognizes that the Spirit is active both inside and outside the church, he goes on to say that Christians should create and nurture the sense of a true community of faith with those outside the church "through activity for coming closer," "activity expressed through dialogue, contacts, prayer in common, investigation of the treasures of human spirituality, in which, as we know well, members of these religions are not lacking" (no. 9).[44]

It is interesting to note here that the *badaliyya* movement, a movement founded by Massignon in 1934, of which Pope Paul VI was a member, "acknowledged a community of faith with Muslims based on a doctrine of the Holy Spirit in Islam."[45]

A CHRISTIAN THEOLOGY OF ISLAM

By conflating the insights of Islamicists like Massignon and of theologians like Rahner, it is possible to see the making of a Christian theology of Islam. Such a theology should try to give a privileged place to Islam, since it is a monotheistic religion not unrelated to the Judeo-Christian tradition. Islam could come to be seen as the general or extraordinary way of salvation for those who, through it, have access to divine transcendence; as one of the best expressions of the worship of God by way of total submission to its own revelation; or, as the historical mediation, granted in God's mercy, of access to grace, through Abraham, the forefather of Jews, Christians, and Muslims.

Vatican II was greatly influenced by such thinking. In speaking of Islam, *Lumen Gentium* said that God's "plan of salvation includes those who acknowledge the Creator. In the first place among these are the Muslims, who, professing to hold the faith of Abraham, along with us, adore the one and merciful God" (no. 16). *Nostra Aetate* (no. 3) assured Muslims that the Catholic church looks upon them "with esteem." It also highlighted the common beliefs of the two religions: Muslims, like Christians, "adore the one God, living and enduring, merciful and all-powerful, Maker of heaven and earth and Speaker to men," even though Christians and Muslims hold a different view of God's oneness. Of the Muslim beautiful names for God, *Nostra Aetate* quoted those that are substantially identical with the names attributed to God by Christians and that resonate with Muslim religious sensitivity. For to say that God is "living and enduring" means, at the same time, that God is personal. When *Nostra Aetate* recalled that God is "merciful and all-powerful," it affirmed that God's mastery over everything is tempered by God's mercy, and that if this mastery is at the origin of the creation of heaven and earth, then mercy has brought God to speak to humankind, presumably through prophets. Thus the council implicitly recognized that Islam is the fruit of a personal divine word, and therefore willed by God.

In *Nostra Aetate*, as in *Lumen Gentium*, Vatican II attempted to link the fundamental Muslim attitude of total submission to God's will to the Abrahamic tradition when it said that Muslims "strive to submit wholeheartedly to God's inscrutable decrees, just as did Abraham, with whom the Islamic faith is pleased to associate itself" (no. 3). However, the texts of *Lumen Gentium* and *Nostra Aetate* are ambiguous, since what the two documents stated is that Muslims "profess to hold the faith of Abraham" (*Lumen Gentium*, no. 16) and "associate themselves with the faith of Abraham" (*Nostra Aetate*, no. 3). According to Thomas Michel:

> Both phrases leave open the possibility for a "restrictive" interpretation which would hold that although Muslims consider themselves in the line of faith of Abraham, in fact we as Christians do not consider them as such.[46]

However, Pope John Paul II clarified this ambiguity in his discourse to the Catholic community in Ankara (3 December 1979) when he said unequivocally, "They have, like you, the faith of Abraham in the one, almighty, and merciful God."[47] In his message to the president of Pakistan (23 February 1981) John Paul II referred to Abraham, "to whose faith Christians, Muslims and Jews eagerly link their own."[48] And in Lisbon (14 May 1982) he said, "And Abraham, our common forefather, teaches all— Christians, Jews and Muslims—to follow the path of mercy and love."[49]

In the pope's acknowledgment that Judaism, Christianity, and Islam are three parallel expressions of the faith of Abraham, he responded to the invitation of the Qur'an to find a formula for uniting the People of the Book under one God: "O People of the Book! Let us come together upon a formula which is common between us—that we shall not serve anyone but God" (Q 3:64). In Muslim perspective, to further promote this union the term "Judeo-Christian tradition" should be changed to the "Judeo-Christian-Islamic tradition." This change would recognize "the symbiotic and highly creative relations among Jews, Christians and Muslims in Southern Spain and other parts of Europe" in the Middle Ages.[50] Chapter 1 above described some of these fruits.

In any event, as Jacques Dupuis points out, the pope's acknowledgment that Judaism, Christianity, and Islam are three parallel expressions of the faith of Abraham is "an implicit admission that Muslims are saved in their own way as heirs of the faith of Abraham."[51] For "just as the Mosaic covenant is still in force for the Jews, so also the faith of Abraham . . . retains its validity."[52] This admission is in keeping with the teaching of *Nostra Aetate* (no. 4) on the role of the patriarchs in salvation and with the teaching of Paul that "the gifts and the calling of God are irrevocable" (Rom 11:29).

Moreover, John Paul II, in his address to young Muslims at Casablanca (19 August 1985), made it explicit that Muslims are not Ishmaelites or Hagarenes to be excluded from the covenant, not heretics or schismatics, but members of a community of faith with Christians: "Your God and ours is the same, and we are brothers and sisters in the faith of Abraham."[53]

The documents of Vatican II recognized the mystery of Islam in God's plan of salvation. John Paul II recognized that both Muslims and Christians are children of Abraham, as did Massignon and Pope Gregory VII before him. In accepting Abraham as their common father in faith, Abraham does not replace Jesus, since only faith in Jesus as the risen Lord makes Christians children of Abraham. As Paul says, "If you belong to Christ, then you are Abraham's offspring, heirs according to the promise" (Gal 3:29). Neither does Abraham replace the Qur'an, for the Qur'an is necessary to make the religion of Abraham concrete for the Muslim community. Members of each community are children of Abraham according to their own self-understanding. And on a more sober note, being children of Abraham does not exempt Christians and Muslims from disputes, conflicts, and misunderstandings. These things do occur among brothers and sisters in a normal family.

JESUS, MUHAMMAD, AND THE QUR'AN

The Catholic church settled the question of the legitimacy of Islam after Christianity but provided no explicit answer to two questions: Was Muhammad a prophet? and Is the Qur'an the word of God? In attempting to make an estimate of Muhammad's prophethood, let us recall the historical background of the birth of Islam. Christianity at the time of the birth of Muhammad was oppressive. There was no Arabic translation of the New Testament available during Muhammad's lifetime.[54] What he heard of the gospel was filtered to him through controversy. Moreover, the distinction between orthodoxy and heresy was closely linked with ethnic and cultural differences. The church had failed to make provision for cultural diversity among Christians. What the church failed to do in the Middle East was Muhammad's finest achievement. He gave to the people of Arabia a divine revelation in their own language and from the lips of one of their own people (Q 26:192, 195). What is remarkable about this revelation is not that it rejected the Western formulations of the divinity of Christ, but that it portrayed Jesus in a manner more in keeping with the intellectual categories and cultures of the Middle East.

What is the Qur'anic view of Jesus? Since Muhammad recognized the revelation of Jews and Christians as God-given, it should surprise no one that the Qur'an speaks of Jesus in glowing terms. In fact, like Catholic Christianity, it teaches a doctrine of the sinlessness of both Jesus and Mary (Q 3:36) and acknowledges his extraordinary birth by a virgin mother (Q 3 and 19). It does so, however, as a sign not of his divinity but of God's omnipotence. It affirms also that Jesus was able to work miracles (e.g., Q 5). It recognizes him as the Messiah (e.g., Q 3:45), who will return at the end of time (Q 4:159), but denies his death and resurrection (Q 4:156:58). For the Qur'an, Jesus is a prophet.

The Islamic denial of Jesus' divinity, death, and resurrection is integrated into the whole theological conception of the Qur'an. The basis of this denial is the rejection of the view that the Fall of Adam not only had dire consequences for him, but that it contaminated and depraved the nature of all humankind. This understanding of Adam's transgression, enshrined in Augustine's interpretation of original sin, became normative for Western Christian theology (both Catholic and Protestant) and included the belief that human sinfulness cannot simply be forgiven but must be atoned for by the death of a sinless person.

The Qur'an teaches that our first parents sinned (Q 2:34) and that all men and women are sinners (Q 4:32; 7:178; 57:21), but it does not teach that the sin of our first parents resulted in the condemnation of every human being born into the world. As Khalifa Abdul Hakim, a Muslim theologian, observes: to Muslims it is completely incongruous that a merciful and compassionate God will damn all humanity to the end of time, "ordaining ineradicable sin for countless children yet unborn and then conceiving as the only means of their salvation that His only son should suffer and be sacrificed to atone for the sins neither He nor others had committed."[55] For Muslims, God is merciful and compassionate. People do sin, yet they have the opportunity to reconcile themselves to God through repentance. In this Muslim attitude to sin we hear echoes of the story of the Prodigal Son.

In not accepting the doctrine of original sin, Muslims cannot accept the Christian remedy for sin proposed by Augustine and his followers. They do so by denying that Jesus died on the cross. They maintain that at the crucifixion Jesus was miraculously "taken up" into heaven and another victim was substituted for him on the cross. (There is no belief in his resurrection for this would imply an acceptance of his crucifixion.) Muslims also deny that Jesus died on the cross because this would imply a failure on God's part to vindicate his prophet.

In dialogue with Christians, Muslims ask, If God did not allow Abraham to sacrifice his son, why would God permit the sacrifice of Jesus, all the more if Jesus is God's son? The denial of the historical actuality of the death of Jesus on the cross still leaves Muslims with a Jesus who was ready to die, a Jesus who was a perfect Muslim, that is, one who was ready to submit totally to the will of God, even unto death. Muslims still see in the will to crucify Jesus a measure of the sin of the world, which is in large measure the message of the cross.[56]

In dialogue with Muslims today Christians should be aware that there are other forms of Christian theology that have a more positive understanding of human nature after the Fall than that found in the Augustinian tradition. This is particularly true of the Eastern fathers[57] who, while affirming the universality of sin, like Muslims, did not connect it with the Fall. When they wrote of the Fall, they represented it as the beginning of sin, as the model or prototype of sin, rather than as the cause of human sinfulness. They did not derive from it any hereditary taint or imputation of guilt to all humanity. For example, Irenaeus, in contrast to Augustine, "pictures Adam and Eve in the Garden of Eden as children; and their sin is accordingly not presented as a damnable revolt, but rather as calling forth God's compassion on account of their weakness and vulnerability."[58]

Christians should also be aware that many contemporary Western theologians,[59] especially Rahner,[60] reject the notion that original sin is simply the sinful act of the first man or is a matter of collective guilt. These views, they hold, cannot be sustained biblically or theologically.

Since there is an intimate connection between the doctrine of the Fall and the Atonement, Christians should not be surprised to learn that many contemporary theologians[61] cannot believe that God must be appeased or propitiated by the blood of the cross before God can forgive. For them, this understanding of the Atonement attributes the crucifixion to God's vindictiveness rather than to human cruelty. They point out that instead of passively accepting punishment in humanity's place, Christ freely accepted the execution the world thrust on him. His death on the cross is an expression of his love for us, though we are sinners, not an expiation demanded by a vindictive God for human sin committed in the cradle of creation. The cross is the school of penitence for the human race. In looking upon Christ's death on the cross, we become ashamed of our own sinfulness and seek amendment of life.

Whatever criticism may be leveled against this understanding of the Atonement, it is free from crude ideas of ransom, satisfaction, substitution, and so on, and it casts no shadow on the character of God. Moreover, it resonates with the Islamic interpretation of the crucifixion, as we have seen. We can thus say that the Muslim-Christian dialogue on the Fall and the Atonement can encourage Christians to acquaint themselves with aspects of their own tradition developed in another part of the church or at another period of the church's history.

Though the Islamic view that Jesus was no more than a prophet differs from the Christian view that he was divine, Islam knows Jesus, recognizes Jesus, and venerates Jesus, to the extent that Muslims, like Christians, look forward to his second coming.

Was Muhammad a prophet? Keeping in mind the teaching of Paul that there will be authentic prophets after Jesus (1 Cor 14:29, 39; 12:10, 28; Rom 12:6), the fact that prophets usually speak at moments of crisis, and that "God can, if He pleases, send witnesses to those who have not been able to see the uplifting manifestation of Christ in the face which we have made bloody with our sins or in the seamless robe which we have torn by our divisions"[62]; keeping in mind the admission of Vatican II that Islam is part of God's plan of salvation and its exhortation to Christians to look upon Muslims "with esteem"; keeping in mind also Pope John Paul II's assertion that the Christian and Islamic revelations are parallel expressions of monotheism and his further admission that Muslims and Christians form a community of faith, then it is possible for Catholics to accept that Muhammad had a prophetic charism that enabled him to communicate some fundamental and biblical truths about God and human beings. Given that before the birth of Islam Christianity was unwilling or unable to formulate who Christ is in categories intelligible to peoples of the non-Western world, then whatever Muhammad may have said with which we do not agree God could have permitted for the good of the world. For it is a Christian principle that "by their fruits you shall know them" (Mt 7:16, 20), and Islam certainly has brought to millions of non-Western peoples a better life, a better knowledge of the one God than they would otherwise have had. Islam may even be said to have helped lapsed Christians to sanctity, as was the case with de Foucauld and Massignon.

When Cardinal Tarancon, president of the Spanish Bishops' Conference, spoke at the 1977 International Muslim-Christian Conference at Cordoba, he called on Christians to recognize, as did the Patriarch Timothy of Baghdad (d. 823) twelve hundred years ago, that "Muhammad walked in the path of the prophets."[63] Cardinal Tarancon put it this way:

> How is it possible to appreciate Islam and Muslims without showing appreciation for the Prophet of Islam and the values he promoted? Not to do this would not only be a lack of respect to which the [Vatican] Council exhorts Christians, but also neglect of a religious factor of which account must be taken in theological reflection and religious awareness.[64]

Timothy's insight was ignored over the centuries because of the Christian polemic against Islam. Today, however, a growing number of Christian scholars, both Catholic[65] and Protestant,[66] join Cardinal Tarancon in recognizing Muhammad as a genuine prophet of God.

And what about the second question concerning the status of the Qur'an as revelation, to which the council gave no explicit answer? Catholics cannot say that the Qur'an is *the* word of God, since for them the term refers to Christ. But they can say that if Muhammad was a prophet in some sense, then the Qur'an is certainly *a* word of God. Moreover, such a view would be in keeping with the thinking of contemporary theologians that revelation is simultaneously the self-communication of God and human response, and that human response is always conditioned by history and culture. It would also be in keeping with Pope John Paul II's theology that the Holy Spirit is at work in the world religions, a point Pope Paul VI also acknowledged with particular reference to Islam.

The view that Jesus is the fullness of the revelation of God, a view based on special revelation, should not prevent Christians from admitting that God's self-revelation continues through prophets after the Christ event, for according to general revelation God has revealed Godself from the beginning of humanity and will continue to do so to the end of time.[67]

Finally, if the Qur'an is a word of God, it must be a word of God not only for Muslims but also for Christians. The Qur'anic revelation can remind the church that if Christ is to be known in the world, he must be presented to people in categories that are intelligible from within their own culture. As Rahner observes:

> The actual concrete activity of the church in its relation to the world outside of Europe was in fact . . . the activity of an export firm which exported a European religion as a commodity it did not really want to change but sent throughout the world together with the rest of the culture and civilization it considered superior.[68]

This was true in the Middle East even before the birth of Islam, as we have seen. It was true in the seventeenth century when Jesuit missionaries, following the initiatives of Matteo Ricci (1552-1610) in China and Roberto de Nobili (1577-1656) in India, tried to inculturate the faith in the non-Western world, for their effort was terminated by order of Pope Benedict XIV in the middle of the eighteenth century. In the twentieth century, as Pope Paul VI admits in his apostolic exhortation *Evangelii Nuntiandi* (no. 20), "the split between the Gospel and culture is without doubt the tragedy of our time."

This need to inculturate the faith in all cultures can be met, because Christianity is a religion based on a living response to a person rather than on giving intellectual assent to propositional truths formulated in Greek and Latin categories by the ecumenical councils of the fourth and fifth centuries. Words such as *substance, essence, nature, person,* and *hyposta-*

sis did not work in explaining the doctrines of the Incarnation and the Trinity to the people of the Middle East, and they do not work today even for Western Christians. This is evident from the fact that a growing number of Christians no longer accept that Christ is both human and divine.[69] As for the doctrine of the Trinity, they find it virtually meaningless. Even Rahner concedes "that Christians, for all their orthodox profession of faith in the Trinity, are almost just 'monotheist' in their actual religious existence." He goes on to add that one "might almost dare to affirm that if the doctrine of the Trinity were to be erased as false, most religious literature could be preserved almost unchanged throughout the process."[70]

In preparing the church to fulfil its mission in the modern world, Vatican II conceded that the church must learn to experience and express itself through the cultural riches not only of Western peoples but of all peoples (*Ad Gentes*, nos. 6-9). It was aware that the church can no longer maintain the integrity of its faith in splendid isolation from the faith of others. It was also aware that the Holy Spirit is at work both inside and outside the visible church. It even acknowledged that though the church is holy, it is "always in need of being purified" (*Lumen Gentium*, no. 8).

As members of that community in need of being purified, we need the perspectives of others, for it is in our encounters with others that we learn who we are. It is through their surprising questions and constant probings that we come to a deeper understanding of what we really believe. In the words of *Gaudium et Spes*, the views of others "can stimulate the mind to a more accurate and penetrating grasp of the faith" (no. 62). Hence the dialogue with Islam is not a threat but an opportunity for us to be more authentic Christians.

Having established the legitimacy of Islam after Christianity, of Muhammad after Jesus, and of the Qur'an after the gospels, the question now is this: Can Christians and Muslims work together to build a new world? The following chapter is devoted to this issue.

Questions for Discussion

1. How would you account for the negative Christian image of Islam over the centuries?

2. Why did irenic Christian voices against this negative attitude go unheard until the twentieth century?

3. Why did Christian theologians in the past try to exclude Muslims from the Abrahamic covenant?

4. Why do many Christians today accept Muslims as children of Abraham?

5. What is the difference in the Christian understanding of revelation before and after Vatican II?

6. How do Christian and Muslim thinkers understand general and special revelation?

7. Why does Islam not teach that one must be a Muslim to be saved?

8. What is the teaching of Vatican II concerning the salvation of non-Christians?

9. Evaluate the Christian theology of Islam presented in this chapter.

10. Is Islam part of God's plan of salvation?

11. Is Muhammad a prophet?

12. Is the Qur'an a word of God?

13. What is the Qur'anic view of Jesus?

14. Is there a doctrine of original sin in Islam?

15. Why do Muslims not accept the Christian doctrine of the Atonement?

16. How is the denial of Jesus' divinity, death, and resurrection integrated into the whole theological conception of the Qur'an?

17. Should the view that Jesus is the fullness of the revelation of God prevent Christians from admitting that God continues to reveal Godself through prophets after the Christ event?

18. If Muhammad were born in a country far from Europe, for example in Indonesia, how would this have affected the place of Islam in world history?

19. To what extent does geography as well as history influence our understanding of salvation?

20. If you are a Christian, how would you explain the doctrines of the Incarnation and the Trinity to a Muslim?

21. What are the benefits of Christian-Muslim dialogue?

Suggested Readings

Abbott, Walter M., ed. *The Documents of Vatican II.* New York: America Press, 1966.

Basetti-Sani, Giulio. *Louis Massignon (1883-1962): Christian Ecumenist.* Edited and translated by Allan Harris Cutler. Chicago: Franciscan Herald Press, 1974.

Brown, Stuart E., trans. *The Challenge of the Scriptures: The Bible and the Qur'an.* Maryknoll, N.Y.: Orbis Books, 1989.

Daniel, Norman. *Islam and the West: The Making of an Image.* Edinburgh: Edinburgh University Press, 1960.

Dulles, Avery. *Models of Revelation.* Garden City, N.Y.: Doubleday, 1983.

Dupuis, Jacques. *Jesus Christ at the Encounter of World Religions.* Maryknoll, N.Y.: Orbis Books, 1991.

Gaudeul, Jean-Marie. *Encounters and Clashes: Islam and Christianity in History.* Vol. 1. Rome: Pontificio Istituto di Studi Arabi e Islamici, 1990.

Haddad, Yvonne Yazbeck, and Wadi Zaidan Haddad, eds. *Christian-Muslim Encounters.* Gainesville, Fla: University Press of Florida, 1995.

Kuschel, Karl-Josef. *Abraham: Sign of Hope for Jews, Christians, and Muslims.* New York: Continuum, 1995.

Parrinder, Geoffrey. *Jesus in the Qur'an.* London: Faber and Faber, 1965.

Watt, W. Montgomery. *Muslim-Christian Encounters.* London and New York: Routledge, 1991.

4

Facing the Future

MUSLIMS

In Muslim perspective the way forward in Muslim-Christian relations rests on the Christian recognition that both Christianity and Islam are ways of salvation. "For," as Mohamed Talbi asks, "what chance is there for an open-minded dialogue free from distrust if, from the very beginning," one side lays down "the absolute principle that those of the other side will inevitably be condemned to hell solely on account of their convictions?"[1] In this regard, as we recall, though Muslims regard the Qur'an as the final and definitive revelation of God, they emphasize that the Qur'an makes no exclusivist claim that the acceptance of its revelation is necessary for salvation. For the Qur'an the many religions can be ways of salvation:

For each one of you We have appointed a Law and a Way of conduct. If God had so willed He would have made you all one community. But it is His wish to test you in what He has given you; so compete in goodness. To God shall you all return and He will tell you about what you have been disputing (Q 5:48).

Even when replying to the Jewish and Christian claims that salvation comes through acceptance of their particular revelation (Q 2:113; 2:111; 3:120), the Qur'an says: "Whoever surrenders himself to God while he does good deeds as well, he shall find his reward with his Lord, shall have no fear, nor shall he come to grief" (Q 2:112). Elsewhere the Qur'an explicitly acknowledges that Christians are saved through their own revelation, "Surely those who believe [that is, Muslims] and those who are Jews, and Christians and Sabaeans—whoever believes in God and the Last Day and does what is right—shall be rewarded by their Lord; they have nothing to fear or to regret" (Q 2:62). The Qur'an even goes as far as to say, "You will find the nearest of all people in friendship to the Believers [that is, Muslims] those who say they are Christians" (Q 5:82).

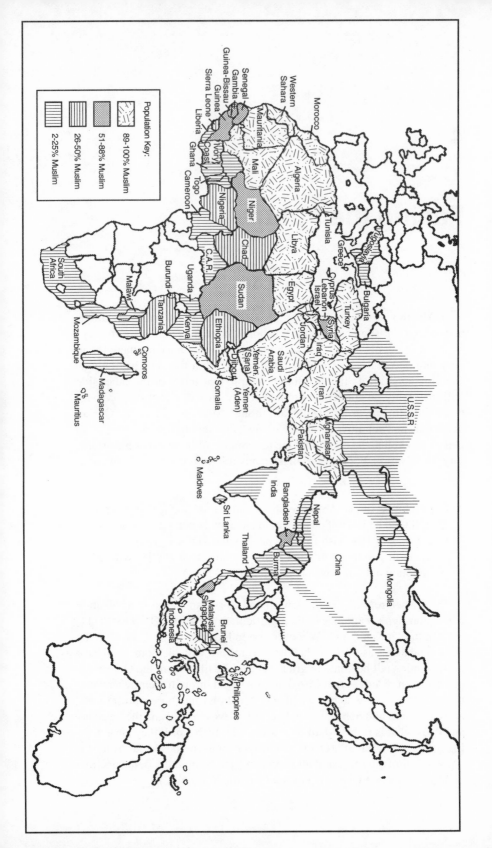

Main Concentration of Muslims in the Contemporary World

Population Key:

89-100% Muslim

51-88% Muslim

26-50% Muslim

2-25% Muslim

Western Sahara
Morocco
Senegal
Gambia
Guinea-Bissau
Guinea
Sierra Leone
Liberia
Ivory Coast
Ghana
Togo
Cameroon
Mauritania
Mali
Nigeria
Niger
Algeria
Libya
Chad
C.A.R.
Uganda
Burundi
Tanzania
Malawi
South Africa
Mozambique
Madagascar
Mauritius
Comoros
Kenya
Ethiopia
Somalia
Djibouti
Egypt
Tunisia
Greece
Cyprus
Lebanon
Israel
Syria
Jordan
Iraq
Turkey
Bulgaria
Yugoslavia
Saudi Arabia
Yemen (Sana)
Yemen (Aden)
Iran
Afghanistan
Pakistan
India
Maldives
Sri Lanka
Bangladesh
Nepal
Thailand
Burma
China
Mongolia
U.S.S.R.
Malaysia
Singapore
Brunei
Indonesia
Philippines
Sudan

The Islamic understanding of mission follows from the teaching of the Qur'an that divergent revelations can lead to salvation. Thus, as Mohamed Talbi,[2] Khalid Duran,[3] and Riffat Hassan[4] explain, for Muslims mission does not mean proselytism, though it does not exclude it, but rather an invitation to faith through witness and proclamation. They stress that the Qur'an reminds the Prophet Muhammad himself that he should not feel responsible if people refuse to accept the message, for it is God who guides to Godself those whom God chooses: "Thou guidest not whom thou likest, but God guides whom He will, and knows very well those who are guided" (Q 28:56). The mission of Muslims is to give witness to the Qur'anic faith. It is for God to convert people: "Thus We appointed you a midmost nation that you might witness to the people, and that the Messenger might be a witness to you" (Q 2:143).

For Muslims, mission as proclamation includes dialogue with those of other faiths, for as the Qur'an says: "Call thou to the way of the Lord with wisdom and good admonition, and dispute with them in the better way" (Q 16:125). The importance of dialogue with people of the biblical religions is specially noted: "Dispute not with People of the Book save in the fairer manner, except for those of them that do wrong; and say: 'We believe in what has been sent down to us, and what has been sent down to you; our God and your God is one, and to Him, we have surrendered'" (Q 29:46).

The acceptance of a plurality of ways of salvation does not lead Muslims to a comfortable quietism or to the belief that the many ways of salvation are equal. This is clear from the fact that the Qur'an insistently calls people to Islam as the final message from God that confirms and completes all the scriptures which preceded it. Others are invited to become Muslim, for Muslims are "the best of peoples evolved for mankind, enjoying what is right, forbidding what is wrong, and believing in God" (Q 3:110). Effective mission through dialogue calls for commitment, yet dialogue is as much a question of self-respect as of respect for others. Conversion to Islam should take place without pressure of any kind. There should be "no compulsion in religion" (Q 2:256).

When Muslims and Christians recognize that they belong to communities that are ways of salvation, and that both communities have a mission to call the other to faith through witness and dialogue, the way to the future is paved for collaboration. As the Muslim scholar Syed Z. Abedin puts it, our differences define our identity. These "differences should not be in jeopardy in our coming together. But given these distinctions there are wide areas of belief and action where we can fruitfully cooperate and work for the betterment of mankind in service to our common Lord and Creator."[5]

At the Christian-Muslim consultation in 1976 in Chambésy, Switzerland, Khurshid Ahmad, director general of the Islamic Foundation based in the United Kingdom, claimed that the difference between the Islamic understanding of mission and the Muslim experience of Christian mission is at the root of the tensions in the present Muslim-Christian relationship.[6] He observed that since the birth of Islam "Christians and Muslims have lived side by side in the Muslim world, on the whole, in peace and harmony with each other."[7] It was with the arrival of the Christian missionaries in the company of European colonizers that tensions developed.[8] These tensions developed because the prime concern of the Christian missionary enterprise seems to have been the subversion of the faith and culture of Islam. Instead of witnessing to their faith that the fullness of God had appeared in Jesus Christ and convincing others of this by words and deeds of love, the missionaries engaged in unfair practices to convert Muslims to Christianity. For example, they targeted the poor, the sick, and the immature and offered them economic assistance, medical aid, and education. In Muslim experience Christian mission was not something holy and noble.

Ahmad further observed that under colonialism Christians had no desire to enter into interreligious dialogue or collaboration. Now that the age of colonialism is over, Muslims wonder if the present Christian interest in dialogue is not a postcolonial ruse to undermine their faith. They are suspicious that Christians interested in dialogue are really in competition with Muslims for converts, since many Christians in the West look upon the revival of Islam as anathema. If Christians do not recognize Islam as a way of salvation, Muslims ask, what is their motive for wanting to engage in dialogue and collaboration?

In spite of their mistrust of the Christian motive for dialogue, Muslims do recognize the need for dialogue in our increasingly interdependent world. But here again they face the problem that Christians are better prepared than they are for dialogue. On the one hand, they know that in each age the pressure of contestation has forced Christian theology to ponder its own values, respond to challenges, and even be enriched by elements compatible with its own worldview. On the other hand, they are keenly aware that Muslim theology has progressively lost contact with developments in the world since the Middle Ages. The unequal preparedness of the Muslim and Christian worlds to face the challenges of the modern world is a reason why Muslims living in the Muslim world do not initiate dialogue and are often hesitant to enter into dialogue initiated by Christians. Their unpreparedness also explains why there is no one international organization for promoting dialogue with Christians.

However, Muslim scholars (such as Hasan Askari, Khalid Duran, Abdullahi Ahmed An-Na'im, and Mohamed Talbi)[9] who have been exposed to Western thought acknowledge that the adventure of dialogue with Christians "is less perilous than becoming more rigid in one's attitudes and fighting to defend frontiers in a world where frontiers are becoming more and more an anachronism."[10] Talbi, speaking for these scholars, claims:

The dividing lines between different faiths no longer run in the same direction as before. The opposition is not so much between different concepts of God and of the way in which to serve him. A far deeper division has taken place between those who are striving to attain man's destiny without God, and those who can conceive of man's future in and through God.[11]

The threat of secularism has led Muslim and Christian scholars to think that the joint development of a God-centered ethic is the most fertile ground for Christian-Muslim collaboration.[12] The Muslim scholar Ziauddin Sardar put it well when he said: "The fire of secularism burns thoroughly; and postmodernism is ever ready to sweep clean the ashes of all theistic worldviews." This threat makes Christians and Muslims an endangered species. Their "lost ground can only be regained through ethical endeavour, through a joint enterprise that takes God-centered ethics to the very heart of the modern world."[13]

The Qur'an encourages interreligious dialogue on ethical issues and even provides it with a firm doctrinal base: "Help one another in righteousness and piety, but help not one another in sin and rancour" (Q 5:2). This principle allows Muslims to cooperate with Christians, and others, in the development of a global ethic "with a view to creating a climate conducive to the survival of mankind and the attainment of peace and harmony and the enrichment of the quality of life" for all.[14] Participation in the development of a global ethic is "not a concession they condescend to make to the exigencies" of the modern world; "it is the *sine qua non* of their faith existence."[15]

In this God-centered ethic the Christian stress on love must be integrated with the Qur'anic emphasis on justice: "Say: My Lord enjoins justice" (Q 7:29); "God loves those who act in justice" (Q 49:9); "Do justice, it is nearer to piety" (Q 5:8). The New Testament concurs: "Not everyone who says to me, 'Lord, Lord,' will enter the kingdom of heaven, but only the one who does the will of my father in heaven" (Mt 7:21). The integration of love and justice must be expressed through praxis. Praxis would ensure that this ethic is concerned with improving the quality of human and ecological life in this world and is not merely a preparation for life in the world to come. The kingdom of God must come on earth as it is in heaven.

Sardar's thinking echoes that of John Paul II when he spoke to the Catholic community in Ankara (3 December 1979):

When I think of this (Islamic) patrimony and of the value it has for man and society, its capacity to offer a direction to life, to fill the void left by materialism, to give a sure foundation to social and juridical organization, I wonder if it is not urgent, precisely today when Christians and Muslims have entered a new period of history, to recognize and develop the spiritual bonds which unite us in order to "safeguard and foster, on behalf of all humankind—as the Council invites us to do—social justice, moral values, peace and freedom" (*Nostra Aetate*, no. 3).[16]

The development of a God-centered ethic is not self-righteous, since it has to show "in terms of policies and options, and where possible by practical demonstration, how good can be attained."[17] Above all, it has to find a solution to the contentious issue of human rights for all, regardless of their religion. In this connection Westerners need to remind themselves that in many settings Muslims do not enjoy the same rights as Christians. For example, the public does not always recognize Muslim religious holidays. Dietary restrictions and dress codes often pose difficulties for Muslims in public schools and in job promotion. Chaplaincy programs in prisons and hospitals and in homes for the aged do not always ensure that the religious services and dietary provisions are suitable to the residents' religious practices. Such behavior not only undermines the cherished principle of collaboration, but it harms the prospects for full religious freedom for Christians who live as minority communities elsewhere in the world.

A God-centered ethic that respects the rights of all would be a joint step by the two largest families of believers to be faithful to the God of Abraham, Isaac, and Ishmael, to the God of the Bible and the Qur'an, to the God who acts in history.

In sum, for Muslims the way forward in Muslim-Christian relations rests on the Christian acceptance of Islam as a way of salvation, the understanding of mission as an invitation and witness to faith, and the advancement of dialogue as a respectful exchange of ideas that leads to collaboration in the promotion of the kingdom of God.

PROTESTANTS

In 1948, when the changed circumstances of the postcolonial world challenged Christians to reassess their attitude and relationship to people of other faiths, Protestants established the World Council of Churches (WCC). In 1971, after lengthy internal consultations and discussion among its member churches, the WCC initiated a Program for Dialogue with People of Living Faiths and Ideologies (DFI). The significance of this initiative was emphasized when in 1975 a whole section of the Nairobi assembly was devoted to the theme "Seeking Community: The Common Search of People of Various Faiths, Cultures and Ideologies." However, when the report of the section was presented to the assembly, there was open conflict on the theological meaning of dialogue and its relation to the church's missionary activity.[18]

In response to these fears, the DFI organized a major consultation in Chiang Mai, Thailand, in the spring of 1977; in 1979 it published its *Guidelines on Dialogue,* an attempt to provide a firm theological basis for dialogue.[19] Though it was careful not to say that the various religions can be possible ways of salvation, controversy over the issue of mission and dialogue broke out again at the Vancouver assembly in 1983.

Behind all these debates has been the conviction of exclusivists that the many religions are *not* ways of salvation. Salvation is through faith in Christ alone. Because of this conviction exclusivists saw a conflict between mission and dialogue. They maintained that the churches' encounter with non-Christians should be one of mission with a view to proselytism, not dialogue with a view to collaboration. As Konrad Raiser, a former deputy general secretary of the WCC, observes:

> [For exclusivists] dialogue with people of other faiths, however desirable it might be on purely human grounds in the interest of peaceful coexistence in a society of people with differing religious beliefs, must always remain subordinate to belief in the finality of Christ and the consequent missionary obligation to proclaim the gospel to all.[20]

Those exclusivists who acknowledged the biblical teaching that there is a general revelation of God as well as the special revelation given through Christ argued that general revelation can provide a theological foundation for dialogue and cooperation. However, they nevertheless maintained that it is not possible to know if a general revelation of God is sufficient for salvation. For them, as for all exclusivists, salvation is through the special revelation of God alone.

Although the theological debate concerning mission and dialogue in the WCC is still far from reaching a resolution, Konrad Raiser acknowledges that there are some theologians associated with the WCC itself (for example, Wesley Ariarajah, Stanley Samartha, and José Míguez Bonino)[21] who suggest that the time has come for a shift from an exclusive christocentric paradigm of salvation to a more pluralist model in the interest of interreligious dialogue and collaboration. These theologians claim that a theocentric paradigm, which characterizes the teaching and preaching of Jesus himself, "must be given a fresh emphasis to counter a deeply rooted 'christomonism' which tends to regard Jesus as the Christian God and makes it impossible to have any meaningful dialogue with neighbors of other faiths."[22] For them, a theocentric model of salvation can enable Christians to take the doctrine of the Trinity seriously, and this doctrine teaches that both Christ and the Holy Spirit play a role in the economy of salvation. Salvation is not through Christ alone.

Whatever merit a trinitarian approach to the salvation of non-Christians may have for those who suggest it, it is important to note that there is no one Christian interpretation of the Trinity, and the doctrine itself, in whatever way it is understood, is unworkable for dialogue with Muslims. According to John Hick, trinitarian theories fall into two main groups, "according to whether or not the 'Persons' . . . are thought of as . . . selves in the sense of distinct centers of consciousness and will."[23] If the three "Persons" are persons in this sense, we have a social conception of the Trinity. Hick then observes that Muslims see this social conception of the Trinity as "constitutively an incipient, or even an explicit, tritheism."[24]

The other kind of trinitarian doctrine understands *persona* in the sense of role; the meaning is derived from the mask worn by an actor on the Roman stage to indicate the role he was playing. According to Hick, in this type of trinitarianism

> God is unambiguously one, but is known in three roles or relation-ships of Creator (God the Father), Redeemer (God the Son) and Sanctifier (God the Spirit). Father, Son and Spirit are thus not three distinct but interrelated individuals . . . but symbolize three aspects of the divine nature as differentiated from our human standpoint. God is one and undivided in the divine nature, but is humanly experienced, and therefore humanly thought [of], in these three ways.[25]

Relying on this second understanding of the Trinity many Christians, including John Hick, have claimed that the threefold naming of God is compatible or analogous to the ninety-ninefold Islamic naming of God. They have even suggested that it is possible to "group the ninety-nine Names into three columns corresponding approximately to the three trinitarian names"[26]: Father, Son, and Holy Spirit. Muslims reject this suggestion, for as Muzammil H. Siddiqi asks,[27] why should Muslims group these names into three columns, and not four or five? For him, to limit the columns to three is to impose a Christian understanding of God on Islam. In Islam, the ninety-nine names do not suggest a limit but rather the infinity of God. Furthermore, Muslims do not call God Father, they deny that God had a Son, and for them the Holy Spirit refers to the angel Gabriel.

In spite of the reluctance or inability of the more than three hundred member churches of the WCC to reach consensus on a theological paradigm that would recognize Islam as a way of salvation, and, in turn, would dissipate the tension between mission and dialogue, the DFI has managed to organize two major international Christian-Muslim dialogue meetings. At Broumana, Lebanon (1972), the theme of the meeting was "In Search of Understanding and Cooperation." At Colombo, Sri Lanka (1982), the topic was "Christians and Muslims Living Together: Ethics and Realities of Humanitarian and Development Programs."[28]

At these meetings both Christians and Muslims recognized the need for better relations. For the most part, however, the meetings reflected the reality of conflict between the two communities rather than the promise of engagement. In essence, the Protestants wanted to address the issue of collaboration without conceding that Islam is a way of salvation. The Muslims argued that the Christian acknowledgment of Islam as a way of salvation is the only firm foundation for dialogue and collaboration. The DFI was not prepared to build the future of the Muslim-Christian relationship on such a foundation.[29]

Without resolving the theological issues of salvation, mission, and dialogue, the DFI went on to organize regional meetings. In Porto Novo, Benin (1986), the theme was "Religion and Responsibility;" in Bali, Indonesia (1986), it was "Advancing Together into the Next Century;" in Kolymbari, Greece (1987), it was "Religion and Society;" and in New Windsor, Maryland, U.S.A., it was "The Challenge of Religious Pluralism."[30] These regional meetings, like the international ones, failed to yield tangible results.[31]

At the local level some Protestant organizations that are not dependent on the initiatives of the DFI have an impressive record in promoting Muslim-Christian interaction. For example, in India there is the Henry Martyn Institute for Islamic Studies, and in England the Center for the Study of Islam and Christian-Muslim Relations at the Selly Oak Colleges in Birmingham.

ROMAN CATHOLICS

In contrast to the World Council of Churches, when Vatican II (1962-65) addressed the issue of the salvation of non-Christians, the assessment was positive. Like Islam, *Lumen Gentium* acknowledged that the world religions can be possible ways of salvation and stated explicitly that God's "plan of salvation includes those who acknowledge the Creator. In the first place among these are the Muslims, who, professing to hold the faith of Abraham, along with us, adore the one and merciful God" (no. 16; see also *Nostra Aetate*, no.3).

In an effort to improve the Muslim-Christian relationship, Pope John Paul II went even further. He followed the lead of Vatican II and the Qur'an and attempted to develop a theology of community centered on Abraham. As was pointed out in the previous chapter, in his address to Muslims at Casablanca (19 August 1985) and elsewhere, he made it explicit that Muslims are members of a community of faith with Christians: "Your God and ours is the same, and we are brothers and sisters in the faith of Abraham."[32] In his acknowledgment that Islam and Christianity are parallel expressions of the faith of Abraham, he responded to the invitation of the Qur'an to find a formula for uniting the People of the Book under one God: "O People of the Book! Let us come together upon a formula which is common between us—that we shall not serve anyone but God" (Q 3:64).

According to Jacques Dupuis, the pope's admission that Islam and Christianity are parallel expressions of the faith of Abraham is "an implicit admission that Muslims are saved in their own way as heirs of the faith of Abraham." For "just as the Mosaic covenant is still in force for the Jews, so also the faith of Abraham . . . retains its own validity."[33] This admission is in keeping with *Nostra Aetate* (no. 4) on the role of the patriarchs in salvation and with the teaching of Paul that "the gifts and the calling of God are irrevocable" (Rom 11:29).

In the Abrahamic model of community suggested by Pope John Paul II, and by Pope Gregory VII before him, Abraham does not replace Jesus, since only faith in Jesus as the risen Lord makes Christians children of Abraham. As Paul says, "If you belong to Christ, you are Abraham's, heirs according to the promise" (Gal 3:29). Neither does Abraham replace the Qur'an, for the Qur'an is necessary to make the religion of Abraham concrete for the Muslim community. Christians and Muslims are children of Abraham according to their own self-understanding. Both communities of faith are part of God's plan of salvation. The acceptance of Abraham as the common forefather of both Christians and Muslims is not self-seeking. It facilitates dialogue with Jews and does not exclude dialogue with the adherents of other monotheistic religions, a point that Abraham himself indicated when he accepted a blessing from Melchizedek (Gn 14:18-20) and chose Machpelah as his burial place (Gn 25:9).

The Roman Catholic understanding of mission as an invitation to faith through witness and proclamation follows from the church's teaching that the many religions can be possible ways of salvation and is in harmony with the Islamic understanding of mission. In his encyclical *Redemptoris Missio* Pope John Paul II makes it clear that the purpose of Christian mission is to witness to the special revelation of God in Christ: "The witness of a Christian life is the first and irreplaceable form of mission" (no. 42). The proclamation of the word of God is a Christian responsibility and "is the permanent priority in mission" (no. 44). Conversion to Christianity is "a gift of God. . . . It is the Spirit who opens people's hearts so that they can believe in Christ and 'confess him' (cf. 1 Cor 12:13); of those who draw near to him through faith Jesus says (Jn 6:44): 'No one can come to me unless the Father who sent me draws him'" (no. 46).

For Roman Catholics, as for Muslims, mission embraces dialogue. As *Redemptoris Missio* goes on to say: "Interreligious dialogue is part of the church's evangelizing mission. Understood as a method and means of mutual knowledge and enrichment, dialogue is not in opposition to mission; indeed, it has special links to that mission and is one of its expressions" (no. 55).

Although Vatican II acknowledges that Islam is part of God's plan of salvation, *Redemptoris Missio* emphasizes that this does not lessen the church's "duty and resolve to proclaim without fail Jesus Christ who 'is the way, the truth and the life'" (no. 55). The encyclical insists that effective mission through dialogue calls for commitment: "Dialogue should be conducted and implemented with the conviction that the Church is the ordinary means of salvation and that she possesses the fullness of the means of salvation" (no. 55). Conversion to Christianity, like conversion to Islam, should take place without pressure of any kind. For, as *Dignitatis Humanae*, Vatican II's declaration on religious freedom, declared:

> The human person has a right to religious freedom. . . . All are to be immune from coercion on the part of individuals or of social groups and of any human power, in such wise that in matters religious no one is to be forced to act in a manner contrary to his own beliefs. Nor is anyone to be restrained from acting in accordance with his own beliefs, whether privately or publicly, whether alone or in association with others, within due limits (no. 2).

In mission through dialogue, religious truth should be proposed, not imposed. Both Christians and Muslims should be free to convince and be convinced. Maurice Borrmans, in his *Guidelines for Dialogue between Christians and Muslims,* which was approved by the Vatican, put it this way:

> Believers in dialogue engage in a holy "spiritual emulation" in which they "vie with one another in good works" (Q 5:48), that is, they seek to help each other surpass themselves, to become more closely conformed to the path which the Lord has indicated to them and thus draw closer to Him in the practice of active goodness.[34]

Since Catholics and Muslims recognize that they are both part of God's plan of salvation and share a common understanding of mission, the way to the future is paved for various types of dialogue. There is the dialogue of theological exchange, in which specialists seek to deepen their understanding of their own respective traditions; the dialogue of religious experience, in which even ordinary persons share their life of prayer with one another; the dialogue of action, in which Christians and Muslims collaborate for the integral development of people and struggle to safeguard religious values in the face of the challenge of secularism; and the dialogue of life, in which people who live in pluralistic societies share their common problems and preoccupations and help each other to live according to their faith.[35]

In an effort to prepare Christians to face the future together with Muslims, Pope Paul VI did pioneering work in directing the church to a better understanding of Islam. In 1964 he instituted the Secretariat for Non-Christians (since 1989 called the Pontifical Council for Interreligious Dialogue) to search for methods and ways of opening a suitable dialogue with non-Christians. In keeping with this spirit of openness, every year since 1967 the secretariat, through its president, sends a message on behalf of all Catholics to all Muslims of the world on the occasion of the conclusion of their one-month fast of Ramadan. This is a unique example of a major religion sending a yearly goodwill message to the followers of another major religion.

In addition to instituting the secretariat, in his first encyclical, *Ecclesiam Suam,* Pope Paul VI singled out Islam for special mention among the various religious traditions: "We refer to the adorers of God according to the conception of monotheism, the Muslim religion especially, deserving of our admiration for all that is true and good in their worship of God" (no. 107). And in 1969, on the occasion of the canonization of the Ugandan martyrs, Pope Paul VI met with the Muslims of Uganda and publicly honored the Muslims of that country who had died as witnesses to the faith.

The present pope has met more often with Muslims than any other pope in history. In his pontificate he has addressed Muslim groups more than forty times and has had many private audiences with Muslim religious leaders.[36] Worthy of special mention is John Paul II's visit to Casablanca on 19 August 1985 at the invitation of the King of Morocco, King Hassan II. There the pope addressed eighty thousand youths on the values shared in common by Christianity and Islam as the basis of collaboration in building a new society where God is at the center.[37]

Muslims appreciate what John Paul II has been doing to bring Christians and Muslims together. For example, in March 1991, after the Gulf War, Hamid Algabid, the secretary general of the Organization of the Islamic Conference, wrote a letter to the pope in which he praised the pope's efforts for peace in the Middle East.[38] And at the opening session of the sixth assembly of the World Conference on Religion and Peace, held in November 1994 at the Vatican, Ahmed Muhammad Ali, secretary general of the Muslim World League, publicly thanked the pope for his leadership during the preparatory phase of the United Nations Conference on Population and Development.[39]

On 16 October 1995, in Morocco, at the commemoration of the tenth anniversary of the pope's visit to Casablanca, Cardinal Francis Arinze, the current president of the Pontifical Council for Interreligious Dialogue, spoke glowingly of the meetings, symposia, colloquia, and visits that have been organized by universities, cultural and research centers, religious institutions, and governments to promote Christian-Muslim understanding since the pope's visit.[40] The cardinal gave special thanks to the Ahl al-Bait Foundation in Amman, Jordan, and the World Islamic Call Society in Tripoli, Libya, for collaborating with the Pontifical Council in organizing colloquia in an effort to build bridges of trust and friendship. He reported that the World Muslim League, the World Muslim Congress, the Organization of the Islamic Conference for *Daw'ah* and Relief and Al Azhar University had held a meeting in June 1994 with the Pontifical Council to establish a permanent committee "to discuss matters of common concern and organize colloquia on mutually agreed themes in the future."[41]

Cardinal Arinze acknowledged that though gains have been made in the way forward in Christian-Muslim relations since 1985, these relations have not been as positive in every part of the world. There remains, for example, the painful conflict in Bosnia-Herzegovina, tensions in Somalia, the longstanding war in Southern Sudan, and occasional outbreaks of violence in parts of Nigeria.

Because of the initiatives of Pope Paul VI and Pope John Paul II, many Muslim countries now see the usefulness of maintaining diplomatic relations with the Holy See, not because their governments want to become Christian, but because they are realistic enough to realize the historic place of the Catholic church and the moral contribution the church makes and can make to the world.

Diplomatic relations between Muslim countries and the Vatican have been beneficial to both. For example, when the Vatican established diplomatic relations with Libya in March 1997, it explained its action as a step aimed "at furthering international dialogue and helping Libya take its rightful place in the 'community of nations.'" The Vatican said that "in recent talks the Libyan government had shown cooperation on the issue of religious freedom." Underlining the Vatican's establishment of diplomatic relations with Libya was its hope "that the southern coast of the Mediterranean can become a region of 'peace, stability and security.' Libya's western neighbour is Algeria, where church leaders have been among the victims of violence by Muslim extremists."[42]

Apart from the Holy See, beginning in the 1970s bishops' conferences have sought to promote understanding with Muslims. Examples are the Federation of the Asian Bishops' Conference and the Regional Episcopal Conference of French-Speaking Africa.

Many religious congregations also make a great contribution in promoting mutual understanding between Christians and Muslims: The Missionaries of Africa, also known as the White Fathers, run the Pontifical Institute for Arabic and Islamic Studies in Rome, which publishes two periodicals: the scholarly journal *Islamochristiana,* and the more popularly written *Encounter—Documents for Muslim-Christian Understanding*; the Dominicans have a commitment to this apostolate in Egypt; the Little Brothers and Sisters of Jesus, inspired by the life and work of Charles de Foucauld among poor Muslims in North Africa, continue to edify both Muslims and Christians; and the Jesuits, who run the Pontifical Gregorian University in Rome, have a working relationship with the University of Ankara in Turkey through the exchange of professors. The meeting of Jesuits who work among Muslims held in Tanail, Lebanon, from 9 to 15 April 1996 focused on ways to cooperate with Muslims in building a more just world so that all can live in peace.

Officials of the church have played and continue to play a substantial role in promoting mutual understanding, but as John Paul II reminds us in his encyclical *Redemptoris Missio*, "each member of the faithful and all Christian communities" are called to do so as well (no. 57). In accepting this responsibility many Christians in various parts of the world have chosen to begin with study programs or conferences for the community to serve as vehicles to stimulate and encourage more interaction in daily life. Since 1976 *Islamochristiana* has reported regularly on the progress of dialogue in local situations.[43]

When Christians and Muslims recognize each other as both involved in God's plan of salvation, the options for collaboration come more sharply into focus. Instances of this come from many countries where Christians and Muslims live together. In Pakistan, Muslim and Christian volunteers run a shelter for battered women. In the Philippines, Muslims and Christians have formed organizations to care for the aged, defend squatters, provide schools and clinics in neglected areas, and run fishing cooperatives for the common good. And in Ethiopia, Christian refugee organizations work together with local Muslim groups. In collaborative projects, when Christians and Muslims laugh and cry together as they struggle in a common cause, they learn about each other. Their shared praxis leads them to study and reflection and to prayer in common. They become co-seekers after God in a sharing community of faith.

NORTH AMERICANS

North America is an important arena for Muslim-Christian dialogue because on this continent Islam is not a Middle Eastern religion any more than Christianity is. The two religions are world religions, not limited to one cultural expression or history. The fact that in North America Christians and Muslims come from all parts of the globe allows for new possibilities for dialogue and collaboration.

The first Muslims to come to North America were apparently Moriscos who came with the Spanish invaders of the New World. This makes the Muslim presence in North America as old as the Christian. The first significant presence of Muslims in North America, however, goes back to about 1875, with immigrants from Lebanon, Syria, Palestine, and Jordan. Lacking proficiency in English, they became unskilled laborers in industrial centers or merchants in the Midwest and Northeast. After the fall of the Ottoman Empire at the end of World War I, other Muslims came from the Middle East and the Balkans.

After World War II three movements of people widened the circle of Muslim immigration considerably. The flocking of students from all over the world, the flow of professionals from developing countries, and the flight of refugees from political upheavals contributed to the exponential growth of Islam. Today some sixty nations are represented in the Muslim immigrant communities of North America. Muslim immigrants who came to North America after the Second World War constitute *per capita* the most highly educated Muslims in the world. This is different from Europe, where labor opportunities have been the primary drawing card.[44]

There are about one and one-half million black Americans who are Muslim. Their history goes back to the seventeenth century, when many of the slaves from Africa were Muslim.[45] With the passage of time, their Islamic heritage became a vague memory, and they became Christian. In the 1920s their memory of Islam was rekindled when Noble Drew Ali formed a black organization called the Moorish Science Temple. The purpose of the organization was to protest white supremacy and to develop black self-esteem by finding an identity in the religion of Islam.

When the Moorish Science Temple lost its impetus by the 1930s, Wallace Fard addressed the concerns of the movement, including its orientation to Islam, by founding a group that grew into the Nation of Islam under Elijah D. Muhammad. The Nation of Islam was successful in helping blacks cope with racism and discrimination. However, there was little of Islam in the movement, except its name. The beliefs and practices of Islam were unknown to the group. This is evident from the fact that the success of the Nation of Islam was based on an ideology that saw white society as Satanic and the Christian faith as Satan's religion. Such an ideology is against the teaching of Islam.

In 1975 a major change occurred in the Nation of Islam when Warith Deen Muhammad introduced orthodox Islam to the black community. The struggle of black Americans to be part of the world community of Islam is reflected in the subsequent changes in the name of the community, from the Nation of Islam to the American Bilalian Community (referring to Bilal, Muhammad's first black disciple), to the World Community of Islam in the West and then to the American Muslim Mission. The American Muslim Mission was eventually disbanded in favor of an identity within the universal community of Islam.

In becoming part of the world community of Islam, and in keeping with Islamic teaching, most American blacks who are Muslim no longer regard white people and the Christian faith as Satanic. For the most part, the exceptions are found in a group that is opposed to the move to bring black American Muslims in line with the universal teaching of Islam. This group is led by Louis Farrakhan. He believes that his group is the true successor of the Nation of Islam because it is faithful to the principles of black separation proposed by Elijah D. Muhammad.

The story of the effort of black Americans to find an identity in the religion of Islam is unique since nearly all have come to Islam from Christianity. This explains why the movement stands somewhat apart from the immigrant Muslim communities, though communication between the two groups is growing.

Many Islamic associations exist to help Muslims maintain their Islam. Since 1952 some of these associations have become members of the Federation of Islamic Associations in the United States and Canada. Federation headquarters is in Detroit, Michigan. In 1962 the Muslim Students Association of the United States and Canada was formed to instill Islamic consciousness in Muslim students. Its headquarters is in Plainfield, Indiana. The Muslim Students Association prepared a *Parents' Manual* to help parents raise their children in a secular North American society. The manual advises parents to encourage their children to make friends with children of devout Christian families rather than the children of families with no religious principles: [Muslim children should] "associate with non-Muslim children in whose homes religious values and high standards of behavior are respected and maintained."[46]

A number of alumni of the Muslim Students Association elected to remain in Canada. In 1972 they formed an independent Council of Muslim Communities in Canada (CMCC). The CMCC makes efforts to establish good relations with Christians and Jews. For example, the council collaborated with Christians and Jews to produce a six-part television series entitled "Holy Land, Holy People," which was viewed in Canada in April 1997. Since then, television stations in Poland, Brazil, and Spain have translated and broadcast the series. It was televised in the United States by the Public Broadcasting Service.

A very active organization, rooted in the immigrant community but drawing black American Muslim centers into its membership, is the Islamic Society of North America (ISNA). Founded in 1982, with headquarters in Plainfield, Indiana, this federation includes the Muslim Students Association of the United States and Canada, the Muslim Communities Association, the Association of Muslim Scientists and Engineers, and the Islamic Medical Association.

There are other efforts at nationwide coordination of activities. For example, the Council of Masajid, located in New York City, encourages cooperation among mosques and Islamic centers. Thus the Islamic centers of both the immigrant and black American communities are united in their concern for the nurture of Islam and the need to act together to confront the issues raised for Muslims by the larger community.

The actual number of Muslims in the United States is disputed.[47] Recent estimates put it at between four and six million, with nearly one-third of these in the three states of California, New York, and Illinois. The 1991 census shows over three hundred thousand Muslims in Canada, two-thirds of whom live in Ontario.[48]

The Protestant attitude to Muslims in North America ranges from the dialogical to the conversionist.[49] Organizations that take a dialogical stance include the Duncan Black Macdonald Center for the Study of Islam and Christian-Muslim Relations, located at Hartford Seminary in Connecticut, founded in 1975; the Office of Christian-Muslim Concerns of the

National Council of Christian Churches in the U.S.A., established in 1977, also located at Hartford Seminary; and the Interfaith Office of the Presbyterian Church in Louisville, Kentucky, established a decade later. Muslims, faithful to the teaching of the Qur'an that Christianity is a way of salvation, do collaborate with these organizations on projects and programs for the common good.

Some Protestant groups, while adhering to a christocentric view of salvation, reject the conversion of Muslims as a necessary corollary of dialogue and collaboration. For example, the Reformed Church of America claims that it does not follow from the thesis "outside Christ, no salvation" that Muslims must be a part of the church to be saved. In a 1987 statement it suggested that when Muslims "avail themselves of the Christian offering and receive the Christian into their hearts as friend," they "receive Christ and avail themselves of him. They eat and drink of that fellowship and, through the faithfulness of their Christian friends, Christ is remembered in them."[50]

Other Protestant organizations take an explicit conversionist stance toward Muslims, for example, the Home Mission Board of the Southern Baptist Convention. Their *Beliefs of Other Kinds: A Guide to Interfaith Witness in the United States* and their *Meeting the World: Ministering Cross-Culturally* both have chapters on Islam that make this quite clear. The Zwemer Institute of Islamic Studies in Pasadena, California, also takes a conversionist stance toward Muslims.[51]

The Roman Catholic Church has responded to the Muslim presence in the United States in a spirit of dialogue and collaboration. In Wisconsin, in 1980, the Ecumenical and Interfaith Commission of the Archdiocese of Milwaukee formed an Islamic-Christian Dialogue Group. A similar effort has been made by the Archdiocese of Los Angeles, California. The National Conference of Catholic Bishops and the American Muslim Council have issued joint statements on two occasions. The introduction to the second statement, issued on 1 September 1994, is instructive:

> This statement represents another step in the ongoing relationship between our two organizations. . . . We recall . . . in particular a previous joint statement on religion and terrorism issued April 16, 1993, in the aftermath of the bombing of the World Trade Center in New York . . . ; especially noteworthy were an interfaith appeal for Balkan refugees and a prayer vigil for peace coinciding with the interfaith prayer vigil hosted by Pope John Paul II in Assisi on January 1, 1993.[52]

In addition to the efforts of the Protestant churches and the Roman Catholic Church to promote dialogue and collaboration with Muslims, numerous initiatives have led to the formation of interfaith councils and other forms of interfaith cooperation. For example, in Washington, D.C., an Interfaith Conference made up of Protestants, Roman Catholics, Jews and Muslims was formed in 1978. This organization is involved in social action as well as in theological reflection. Also in Washington, D.C., a Jewish-Christian-Muslim Trialogue Group has existed since 1978. The group, sponsored by the Kennedy Institute of Ethics affiliated with the Jesuit-run Georgetown University, studies issues of common interest to the three religious communities.

The Program of Religion of the Claremont Graduate School in San Diego, California, organized a Jewish-Christian-Muslim "trialogue" in March 1985 entitled "Three Faiths—One God." The papers were subsequently edited and published by John Hick and Edmund S. Meltzer.[53] The Academy for Judaic, Christian, and Islamic Studies of California organized a conference in Los Angeles in December 1991 on "The Abraham Connection: A Jew, Christian, and Muslim in Dialogue." The dialogue was edited and published by George B. Grose and Benjamin J. Hubbard.[54]

Many theological schools and seminaries sponsor seminars, lectures, and panel discussions, with Christian and Muslim participation, on subjects of mutual interest. For example, The Association of Chicago Theological Schools sponsored a conference in Chicago in April 1993 on "Christian-Muslim Relations: Toward a Just World Order."

North American universities are also a locus for promoting dialogue. They are places where freedom of speech stimulates Christian-Muslim exchanges. Muslim professors are numerous, and already there are thousands of Muslim students from home and abroad.

Learned journals contribute to improving Christian-Muslim relations. The most widely known journal in the United States having to do with Islam and Christianity is *The Muslim World*. This publication began in 1911 to serve the missionary enterprise of the church. Since 1967 it has shown its commitment to dialogue by accepting contributions from Muslims. The *Journal of Ecumenical Studies* also publishes articles by Muslims. Isma'il Ragi al Faruqi, a Muslim scholar, served as the journal's associate editor until his death in 1986. Leonard Swidler, the journal's general editor, collected the articles written by Muslim scholars in the journal under the title *Muslims in Dialogue*.[55]

Christians in the United States and Canada are in a better position than Christians in Western Europe to promote dialogue and collaboration, since North Americans do not have a long history of hostility toward Muslims. In fact, one can argue that prior to the confrontation between the United States and the Islamic nations of the Middle East over oil and Iran in the 1970s, a confrontation exacerbated by the Gulf War in the early 1990s, North Americans have paid little attention to the Muslims in their midst.

Moreover, since North Americans cherish religious and cultural diversity, Christians and Muslims on this continent are in a privileged position to develop a novel dialogue on human rights within the national culture. Such a dialogue could provide an example and frame of reference for

Christians and Muslims in other settings where the issues may be more explosive.

THE BRITISH

The first Muslims to come to Britain were from the Indian subcontinent. The East India company recruited seamen into the merchant navy in the late eighteenth and early nineteenth centuries. Arabs followed when ships started recruiting in Aden and Yemen after the opening of the Suez Canal in 1869. Often laid off when their ships docked in Britain, these seamen settled in port cities such as Cardiff, Tyneside, London, and Liverpool. The significant presence of Muslims came after World War II, when British industry recruited workers from the Caribbean, India, and Pakistan, which, before 1971, included Bangladesh. Immigrants from both parts of Pakistan were almost all Muslims, as were a substantial minority from India and the Caribbean. In addition, Muslims came from Cyprus in the aftermath of the 1957 troubles, and from East Africa, especially after Uganda and Kenya introduced a policy of "africanization" in the late 1960s and 1970s.

The number of immigrants increased dramatically in the early 1960s to preempt the Commonwealth Immigration Act of 1962, intended to close the door on automatic entry for Commonwealth citizens. Most of the immigrants in the eighteen months prior to the passage of the Act were from Pakistan. Since the 1970s most newcomers have been refugees rather than economic migrants. This wave of immigration has included Muslims from the Middle East, especially from Lebanon, Palestine, Iraq, and Iran.

The steady growth of Muslims in Britain is reflected in census figures, which record place of birth. According to Jorgen S. Nielsen:

> The first recording of Pakistanis in the census showed approximately 5,000 in 1951, rising to under 25,000 in 1961. Ten years later the figure (now for Pakistan and Bangladesh together), had risen to 170,000, and by 1991 it was 636,000. The 1991 census produced the following figures relating to country of birth: Bangladeshis, 160,000; Pakistanis, 476,000; Indians, 134,000; Malaysians, 43,000; Arabs, 134,000; Turks, 26,000; Turkish Cypriots, 45,000; and sub-Saharan Africans, 115,000, for a total of 1,133,000.[56]

The figures show that Muslims from Bangladesh, India, and Pakistan account for about 70 percent of the total. That is, the public face of British Muslims is South Asian; Arab Muslims, of whom we hear so much, are actually a minority.

The multiplication and consolidation of Muslim communities after 1962 is also shown in the rising number of mosque registrations: "In 1963 thirteen mosques were registered. . . . The number rose steadily, to 49 in 1970, 99 in 1975, 193 in 1980, 314 in 1985, and 452 in 1990."[57] Mosques registered before 1962 provided facilities for worship and for passing on the teaching and practice of Islam to the next generation. Usually the initiative for their establishment arose within local communities. However, as resources, such as personnel and publications, were limited, many communities found it necessary to find sponsors. It is for this reason that a number of Islamic organizations from the immigrants' countries of origin have established branches in Britain.

The following three organizations reflect the views of the Jama'at-i Islami of Pakistan. The UK Islamic Mission, started in 1963, concentrates on education and community work. The Muslim Educational Trust, set up in 1966, provides personnel for the teaching of Islam in state schools outside the regular time table. Its textbook *Islam: Beliefs and Teachings*, written by Ghulam Sarwar in 1980, had sold more than one hundred thousand copies by 1992. The Islamic Foundation, established in 1973, is a center for research and publishing. It specializes in reading materials for children and publishes a newsletter called "Focus on Christian-Muslim Relations." In 1980 it produced *The Muslim Guide: For Teachers, Employers, Community Workers and Social Administrators in Britain.*[58]

The conservative Deobandi movement, from Deoband north of Delhi, operates two seminaries for the training of religious leaders: one was set up in 1975 at Bury, fifty miles from Bradford; the other, in 1982, at Dewsbury, ten miles away. Other conservative reform movements active in Britain are the Barelwi, the Ahl i-Hadith, and the Tablighi Jama'at.

The Islamic Council of Europe, established in 1973, is recognized by the Islamic Secretariat, Jeddah, as the representative body for Muslims in Europe. It seeks to integrate the Muslims of Britain with those of the continent.

There have been attempts to form umbrella organizations to coordinate the activities of British Muslims. The first such attempt was made by the Union of Muslim Organizations (UMO) in 1970. The attempt failed, though the UMO still exists. Other attempts have been made since then, some sponsored by the Saudi-based Muslim World League and one by the Libya-based Islamic Call Society. The Muslim Institute for Research and Planning, founded in 1972, was linked with Iran. In 1991 it set up the so-called Muslim Parliament, which has attracted more attention in the press than it has found support within the Muslim communities.

The immediate spur to Christian reflection on the presence of Muslims in Britain came from the World of Islam Festival held in 1976. Realizing that Christians were spiritually and theologically unprepared for the festival, the British Council of Churches (BCC), to which the Anglican and major Protestant churches belong, took the initiative to help Christians respond positively to the event. They did so by setting up an Advisory Group to consider the relationship of the churches to Islam and Muslims in Britain. The group held its first meeting in 1974; it was chaired by David Brown, Anglican bishop of Guildford.

As a result of the group's work, Brown wrote *A New Threshold: Guidelines for the Churches in Their Relations with Muslim Communities,* published in 1976. In it he expressed the need not only for good relations with Muslims, but also for an inclusive Christology that sees Christ at work both inside and outside the church: "Christ did not come to make God's love and power the exclusive possession of the Church, but to reveal the nature of him who holds all beings in his embrace."[59] For him, when the churches cross the threshold from an exclusive to an inclusive Christology, they "will discover a joy and a glory which are not found in their present interim theologies."[60] In 1977 the BCC Assembly affirmed that "there is much need for Christians to work with those of other faiths along the lines of the Code of Practice outlined in *A New Threshold.*"[61]

The work of the Advisory Group on Islam helped the churches to recognize that Britain had become a multifaith society. This recognition underlined the need for regular interaction between the churches and all non-Christian people—not only Muslims. Consequently, in Britain today the emphasis is on multifaith relations rather than on specifically Muslim-Christian relations.

To promote multifaith interaction, the Advisory Group developed into the Committee for Relations with People of Other Faiths (CRPOF) of the BCC. When CRPOF published *Relations with People of Other Faiths: Guidelines on Dialogue in Britain* in 1981,[62] the General Synod of the Church of England almost unanimously accepted the document. The General Synod of 1981 also asked its Board of Mission and Unity to prepare a report on the theological aspects of dialogue. In 1984 the board produced a document called, rather tentatively, *Towards a Theology of Inter-Faith Dialogue.*[63] The tendency of the document is toward an inclusivist Christology. It states:

> The Triune God is a God who moved in creation into a relationship with all that is created; who, as the Word, is incarnate in Jesus and yet encountered in other places; and who as Holy Spirit, present in the Church and in the lives of baptized Christians, is also active among those of other faiths and cultures. It is the same God whose saving grace is at work outside the Church as well as within it.[64]

The document then hastens to add:

> What would be contrary to the biblical witness would be the abandonment of a defining loyalty to Jesus Christ as the one in whom

God was reconciling the world to himself and any proposal that this message of reconciliation need no longer be offered to those of other faiths.[65]

Churches other than the Church of England have responded to people of other faiths. For example, a subcommittee of the United Reformed Church published *The Local Churches' Approach to Those of Other Faiths* in 1974, and *With People of Other Faiths in Britain: A Study Handbook for Christians* in 1980. The Methodist Church's Working Party on Multifaith Society published *Shall We Greet Only Our Own Family?* also in 1980.

Before 1984 the Roman Catholic Church did not have an organization specifically responsible for relations with people of other faiths, although it was in close contact with the BCC and had unofficial observers on CRPOF. However, since Vatican II, there have been groups within the Catholic church concerned with issues relevant to the adherents of other faiths. For example, the Catholic Commission on Racial Justice, established in 1971, stated in its "Practical Guidelines for the Church in a Multiracial, Multicultural Society" (1978) that seminaries and colleges of education, in accepting responsibility for the future, should "adopt a more positive and practical approach to the study of other faiths, since this is no longer a concern of theoretical interest to the specialist, or of relevance only to the overseas pastor, but a practical concern for priests and teachers in every part of Britain."[66]

The report of the National Pastoral Congress, held in Liverpool in 1980, acknowledged that in Britain today "Christianity is forced to take seriously the witness given by . . . non-Christian religions to the power of God's Spirit."[67] The bishops' response to the report in *Easter People* encouraged a "spirit of dialogue" in the approach to other faiths, and a better knowledge of the background and beliefs of non-Christian immigrants for Christians "can learn from them and at the same time make known to them [their] own belief, the Good News of Jesus Christ."[68]

Since the Roman Catholic Church established its Committee for Other Faiths in 1984, the committee has produced two publications: *Getting to Know People of Other Faiths* and *What the Church Teaches about Other Faiths*. Both publications are available through the Catholic Truth Society in London.

While the work of the churches has been concerned primarily with preparing Christians to respond positively to people of other faiths, there have also been interfaith initiatives. For example, in Glasgow a Sharing of Faiths group has existed since the early 1970s. The Wolverhampton Interfaith Group has encouraged interreligious dialogue since 1974. In the Midlands the Standing Committee of Christians and Muslims organized a conference in Birmingham in 1976. The conference was held partly in the mosque and partly in the United Reformed Church. The theme was "Church and Mosque in Secular Society." In Leeds, Concord promotes interfaith meetings, and since 1977 has organized an annual Jewish-Christian-Muslim conference on a variety of themes. In 1985 the theme was "Religious Minorities and Secular Society in Britain." In 1986 it was "Youth, Community, and Religion." In the Bradford area churches of different denominations combined to form Outreach in 1980. Its aim is to build bridges of understanding and friendship. The Little Sisters of Jesus, who live among Muslims in London and Aston, play a valuable role in interfaith relations.

Muslim organizations have also shown a willingness to make contact with other religious groups at the local level. For example, in the Birmingham area the mosque at Balsall Heath welcomes visitors and has on several occasions hosted a Muslim-Christian conference on issues of topical concern. The Sparkbrook mosque is equally welcoming and has not only held conversations between Muslims and Christians but has also welcomed visitors of other faiths to Muslim celebrations.

At the national level Muslims played a prominent part in the founding of an Interfaith Network in 1987. When it was constituted, Christianity was represented by the Committee for Other Faiths of the Roman Catholic Church and by the Committee for Relations with People of Other Faiths of the British Council of Churches. All the major faiths in Britain were represented. Islam was represented by the Council of Mosques: UK and Eire, the Imams and Mosques Council (UK), the Islamic Cultural Center (London), the Islamic Foundation, the Islamic League (UK), and the World Islamic Mission (UK). The Director of the Islamic Cultural Center was one of the vice-presidents. The Interfaith Network has proved to be a major channel for interfaith cooperation. Both during the Rushdie affair in 1989 and later, during the 1990-91 Gulf crisis and war, the Interfaith Network was a "significant route through which Muslim groups and the churches were able to keep in touch and explain each other."[69]

In British universities Christians and Muslims have ample opportunity for formal dialogue as well as for informal encounter. Moreover, the Islamic Center in Oxford and the Islamic Academy in Cambridge are both aimed at improving Christian-Muslim relations. However, the center most deeply involved with promoting mutual understanding is the Center for the Study of Islam and Christian-Muslim Relations, at the Selly Oak Colleges in Birmingham. It was established in 1976 as a joint venture of Christians and Muslims to explore the living traditions of the two faiths. The staff is made up of Christians and Muslims, as is the student body.

The Center for the Study of Islam and Christian-Muslim Relations is in close touch with the Conference of European Churches, the Roman Catholic Church, the British Council of Churches, and the World Council of Churches. Since its inception it has published a newsletter, and since 1990 it has published the scholarly journal *Islam and Christian-Muslim Relations*. The general editor for the early issues was Christian W. Troll, a Jesuit.

On the level of praxis people in Britain have begun to accommodate themselves to life in a multifaith society. For example, in May 1985 the city of Bradford elected Muhammad Ajeeb lord mayor. Since he was a Muslim, his inaugural service took place in a mosque at which both Muslim and Christian dignitaries were present. The ceremony opened with a quotation from the Qur'an: "Let us help one another in what is good and pious" (Q 5:2). The same year, in July, "Prayer for the Day," the religious program on BBC radio 4, was given by a Muslim for the first time. Since then, many such broadcasts have taken place. In the spring of 1989 Selwyn College at the University of Cambridge initiated Akbar S. Ahmed the first Muslim fellow of the college. Because the college has strong links with the Church of England, at the ceremony a new fellow has to repeat a reference to the Trinity. Aware that this would be an insurmountable obstacle for a Muslim, the "solution was to drop the reference, leaving only the mention of God which would be acceptable to both Christian and Muslim."[70]

If it is becoming obvious that the only kind of meaningful national life is one that is inextricably bound up with the life of people of other faiths, it is also becoming obvious that any theology of religions based on faith must have a common framework which can serve many religious communities. The development of such a theology is a challenge to all believers. Seyyed Hossein Nasr recognized this challenge when he wrote: "There is also the very important task which lies ahead for Muslims to make peace on the theological level, not only on the political level, with other religions."[71]

While the immigrant generations of Muslims continue to look back to the regions and cultures from which they came, Muslims born in Britain are trying to create a British Muslim identity. They are beginning to distinguish among culture, tradition, and Islam, and to see that much of South Asian religiosity is not relevant or transferable to life in Britain. Muslim scholars who write in English self-consciously address the issue. For example, Shabbir Akhtar, in *A Faith for All Seasons*, calls on Muslims to develop an Islamic thought and praxis responsive to the social, intellectual, and religious realities of Britain.[72]

If today Christians are able to affirm that God is at work in the many religions, they need to say so in a way that is acceptable to all faiths. Recent efforts to do so are encouraging. The inclusive Christology of the Church of England's *Towards a Theology of Inter-Faith Dialogue* is intended to persuade its members to enter into dialogue with those of other faiths. However, the very title of the document reminds us that theology is always provisional. Moreover, the document speaks of interreligious dialogue as a "journey through unfamiliar territory."[73] The British Council of Churches' *Relations with People of Other Faiths* also speaks of dialogue as a pilgrimage with others who are seeking a new future.[74]

The images of pilgrimage and journey are hopeful metaphors that are also found in the Vatican II document *Lumen Gentium* (no. 8). They remind Christians that they are children of Abraham still on the road "to the city that has foundations, whose architect and builder is God" (Heb 11:10). In searching for a theology of religions that is acceptable to Muslims, we recall here that the Catholic church went further than the Church of England, the British Council of Churches, and even Vatican II, when Pope John Paul II recognized that Muslims as well as Christians are children of Abraham. In so doing the Catholic church responded to the invitation of the Qur'an to find "a formula which is common between us—that we shall not serve anyone but God" (Q 3:64). In accepting Abraham as the common father in faith of both Christians and Muslims, Abraham does not replace Jesus; neither does he replace the Qur'an. Members of each community are children of Abraham according to their own self-understanding.

A theology of religions centered on Abraham is not self-seeking. It facilitates dialogue with Jews and does not exclude dialogue with the adherents of other monotheistic religions. Against the idolatrous tendencies of our secular world, Christians in an Abrahamic community can witness *with* people of other faiths that there is no god but God. They can also witness *to* people of other faiths what God has done for them in Christ.

Charles Kimball is right when he observes that the way forward in Christian-Muslim relations will surely be difficult, marked by numerous obstacles, detours, and setbacks. But, in the final decade of the twentieth century, Christians and Muslims can see more clearly that they are sojourners together on the way to the future. The ways in which Christians and Muslims choose to travel that road will have profound consequences for both communities and for the world.[75] Fortunately, in Britain, North America, and elsewhere, there are already positive and encouraging signs of cooperation. Patterns of encounter that once alienated are being replaced by new patterns that seek to take into account the mistakes of the past, the needs of the present, and the promises envisioned by the future.

Questions for Discussion

1. In the Muslim perspective, what is the only firm foundation on which to build the future of the Muslim-Christian relationship?

2. What is the Islamic understanding of mission and dialogue?

3. Why are Muslims often hesitant to initiate dialogue with Christians?

4. As Muslims and Christians face the future together, what issues cry out for immediate attention and collaboration?

5. What is the theological stumbling block facing the WCC in its effort to promote Christian-Muslim dialogue?

6. Why is a trinitarian approach to salvation unworkable in Muslim-Christian dialogue?

7. How effective has the WCC been in improving Christian-Muslim relations?

8. How is an Abrahamic model of community more suited for dialogue with Muslims than a christocentric or trinitarian model of salvation?

9. Are there parallels between the Roman Catholic and the Islamic understanding of mission and dialogue?

10. Why is North America an important area for promoting Muslim-Christian dialogue?

11. What are the similarities and differences between the North American and the British Christian-Muslim encounter?

Suggested Readings

Anees, Munawar Ahmad, Syed Z. Abedin, and Ziauddin Sardar. *Christian-Muslim Relations Yesterday, Today, Tomorrow.* London: Grey Seal, 1991.

Borrmans, Maurice. *Guidelines for Dialogue between Christians and Muslims.* New York: Paulist Press, 1990.

Burrows, William R., ed. *Redemption and Dialogue: Reading "Redemptoris Missio" and "Dialogue and Proclamation."* Maryknoll, N.Y.: Orbis Books, 1993.

Johnstone, Penelope. "Christians and Muslims in Britain." *Islamochristiana* 7 (1981): 167-99 and 12 (1986): 181-90.

McCloud, Aminah Beverly. *African American Islam.* New York and London: Routledge, 1995.

Raiser, Konrad. *Ecumenisn in Transition: A Paradigm Shift in the Ecumenical Movement?* Geneva: World Council of Churches, 1991.

Rousseau, Richard W., ed. *Christianity and Islam: The Struggling Dialogue.* Montrose, Pa.: Ridge Row Press, 1985.

Speight, R. Marston. *Christian-Muslim Relations: An Introduction for Christians in the United States of America.* Hartford, Conn.: Task Force on Christian-Muslim Relations, National Council of the Churches of Christ in the USA, 1983.

Swidler, Leonard E. *Muslims in Dialogue.* Lewiston, N.Y.: Edwin Mellen Press, 1992.

World Council of Churches. *Guidelines on Dialogue with People of Living Faiths and Ideologies.* Geneva: World Council of Churches, 1979.

——————. *Meeting in Faith: Twenty Years of Christian-Muslim Conversations Sponsored by the World Council of Churches.* Compiled by Stuart E. Brown. Geneva: World Council of Churches, 1989.

Appendix 1
Important Suras from
the Qur'an

1 The Prologue

Al-Fātihah: Makki

بِسْمِ اللهِ الرَّحْمٰنِ الرَّحِيْمِ ۞

In the name of Allah, most benevolent, ever-merciful.

ALL PRAISE BE to Allah,
Lord of all the worlds,
2. Most beneficent, ever-merciful,
3. King of the Day of Judgement.
4. You alone we worship, and to You
alone turn for help.
5. Guide us (O Lord) to the path that is straight,
6. The path of those You have blessed,
7. Not of those who have earned Your anger,
nor those who have gone astray.

2 THE COW

154. Do not say that those who are killed
in the way of God, are dead,
for indeed they are alive,
even though you are not aware.

وَلَا تَقُولُوا لِمَن يُقْتَلُ فِي سَبِيلِ اللّهِ أَمْوَاتٌ بَلْ
أَحْيَآءٌ وَلَكِن لَّا تَشْعُرُونَ ۝

155. Be sure We shall try you
with something of fear and hunger
and loss of wealth and life
and the fruits (of your labour);
but give tidings of happiness to those who have patience,

وَلَنَبْلُوَنَّكُم بِشَيْءٍ مِّنَ الْخَوْفِ وَالْجُوعِ وَنَقْصٍ مِّنَ
الْأَمْوَالِ وَالْأَنفُسِ وَالثَّمَرَاتِ وَبَشِّرِ الصَّابِرِينَ ۝

156. Who say when assailed by adversity:
"Surely we are for God, and to Him we shall return."

الَّذِينَ إِذَا أَصَابَتْهُم مُّصِيبَةٌ قَالُوا إِنَّا لِلّهِ وَإِنَّا
إِلَيْهِ رَاجِعُونَ ۝

157. On such men are the blessings of God and His mercy,
for they are indeed on the right path.

أُولَٰئِكَ عَلَيْهِمْ صَلَوَاتٌ مِّن رَّبِّهِمْ وَرَحْمَةٌ وَ
أُولَٰئِكَ هُمُ الْمُهْتَدُونَ ۝

158. Truly Safa and Marwa are the symbols of God.
Whoever goes on pilgrimage
to the House (of God), or on a holy visit,
is not guilty of wrong if he walk around them;
and he who does good of his own accord
will find appreciation with God who knows every thing.

إِنَّ الصَّفَا وَالْمَرْوَةَ مِن شَعَآئِرِ اللّهِ فَمَنْ حَجَّ
الْبَيْتَ أَوِ اعْتَمَرَ فَلَا جُنَاحَ عَلَيْهِ أَن يَطَّوَّفَ
بِهِمَا وَمَن تَطَوَّعَ خَيْرًا فَإِنَّ اللّهَ شَاكِرٌ عَلِيمٌ ۝

159. They who conceal Our signs
and the guidance We have sent them
and have made clear in the Book,
are condemned of God and are condemned by those
who are worthy of condemning.

إِنَّ الَّذِينَ يَكْتُمُونَ مَا أَنزَلْنَا مِنَ الْبَيِّنَاتِ وَالْهُدَىٰ
مِن بَعْدِ مَا بَيَّنَّاهُ لِلنَّاسِ فِي الْكِتَابِ أُولَٰئِكَ يَلْعَنُهُمُ
اللّهُ وَيَلْعَنُهُمُ اللَّاعِنُونَ ۝

160. But those who repent and reform
and proclaim (the truth), are forgiven,
for I am forgiving and merciful.

إِلَّا الَّذِينَ تَابُوا وَأَصْلَحُوا وَبَيَّنُوا فَأُولَٰئِكَ أَتُوبُ
عَلَيْهِمْ وَأَنَا التَّوَّابُ الرَّحِيمُ ۝

161. But those who deny, and die disbelieving,
bear the condemnation of God
and the angels and that of all men,

إِنَّ الَّذِينَ كَفَرُوا وَمَاتُوا وَهُمْ كُفَّارٌ أُولَٰئِكَ عَلَيْهِمْ
لَعْنَةُ اللّهِ وَالْمَلَائِكَةِ وَالنَّاسِ أَجْمَعِينَ ۝

162. Under which they will live, and their suffering
will neither decrease nor be respite for them.

خَالِدِينَ فِيهَا لَا يُخَفَّفُ عَنْهُمُ الْعَذَابُ وَلَا
هُمْ يُنظَرُونَ ۝

163. Your God is one God;
there is no god other than He,
the compassionate, ever-merciful.

وَإِلَٰهُكُمْ إِلَٰهٌ وَاحِدٌ لَّا إِلَٰهَ إِلَّا هُوَ الرَّحْمَٰنُ الرَّحِيمُ ۝

Creation of the heavens and the earth,
alternation of night and day,
and sailing of ships across the ocean
with what is useful to man,
and the rain that God sends from the sky enlivening
the earth that was dead,
and the scattering of beasts of all kinds upon it,
and the changing of the winds, and the clouds which remain
obedient between earth and sky,
are surely signs for the wise.

إِنَّ فِي خَلْقِ السَّمَاوَاتِ وَالْأَرْضِ وَاخْتِلَافِ اللَّيْلِ
وَالنَّهَارِ وَالْفُلْكِ الَّتِي تَجْرِي فِي الْبَحْرِ بِمَا يَنفَعُ
النَّاسَ وَمَا أَنزَلَ اللّهُ مِنَ السَّمَاءِ مِن مَّاءٍ فَأَحْيَا
بِهِ الْأَرْضَ بَعْدَ مَوْتِهَا وَبَثَّ فِيهَا مِن كُلِّ دَابَّةٍ
وَتَصْرِيفِ الرِّيَاحِ وَالسَّحَابِ الْمُسَخَّرِ بَيْنَ السَّمَاءِ
وَالْأَرْضِ لَآيَاتٍ لِّقَوْمٍ يَعْقِلُونَ ۝

2 THE COW

If one is obliged by necessity
to eat it without intending to transgress,
or reverting to it, he is not guilty of sin;
for God is forgiving and kind.
174. Those who conceal any part of the Scriptures
that God has revealed, and thus make
a little profit thereby,
take nothing but fire as food;
and God will not turn to them on the Day of Resurrection,
nor nourish them for growth;
and their doom will be painful.
175. They are those who bartered away
good guidance for error, and pardon for punishment:
How great is their striving for the Fire!
176. That is because God has revealed
the Book containing the truth;
but those who are at variance about it
have gone astray in their contrariness.

Piety does not lie in turning your face
to East or West:
Piety lies in believing in God,
the Last Day and the angels,
the Scriptures and the prophets,
and disbursing your wealth out of love for God
among your kin and the orphans,
the wayfarers and mendicants,
freeing the slaves, observing your devotional obligations,
and in paying the zakat and fulfilling a pledge you have given,
and being patient in hardship, adversity,
and times of peril.
These are the men who affirm the truth,
and they are those who follow the straight path.
178. O believers, ordained for you is retribution
for the murdered,
(whether) a free man (is guilty)
of (the murder of) a free man, or a slave of a slave,
or a woman of a woman.
But he who is pardoned some of it   by his brother
should be dealt with equity,
and recompense (for blood) paid with a grace.
This is a concession from your Lord and a kindness.
He who transgresses in spite of it
shall suffer painful punishment.

2 THE COW

250. And when they were facing Goliath and his hordes
they prayed: "O Lord, give us endurance and steady our steps,
and help us against the deniers of truth."
251. By the will of God they defeated them,
and David killed Goliath,
and God gave him kingship and wisdom,
and taught him whatsoever He pleased.
If God did not make men deter one another
this earth would indeed be depraved.
But gracious is God to the people of the world.
252. These are the messages of God.
We recite them to you in all truth,
as indeed you are one of the apostles.
253. Of all these apostles
We have favoured some over the others.
God has addressed some of them,
and the stations of some have been exalted over the others.
And to Jesus, son of Mary, We gave tokens,
and reinforced him with divine grace.
If God had so willed
those who came after them would never have contended
when clear signs had come to them.
But dissensions arose,
some believed, some denied.
And if God had willed
they would never have fought among themselves.
But God does whatsoever He please.

O believers, expend
of what We have given you
before the day arrives
on which there will be no barter,
and no friendship or intercession matter,
and those who are disbelievers will be sinners.
255. God: There is no god but He,
the living, eternal, self-subsisting, ever sustaining.
Neither does somnolence affect Him nor sleep.
To Him belongs all
that is in the heavens and the earth;
and who can intercede with Him except by His leave?
Known to Him is all that is present before men
and what is hidden
(in time past and time future),
and not even a little of His knowledge can they grasp
except what He will.
His seat extends over heavens and the earth,

2 THE COW

and He tires not protecting them:
He alone is all high and supreme.
256. There is no compulsion in matter of faith.
Distinct is the way of guidance now from error.
He who turns away from the forces of evil
and believes in God, will surely hold fast
to a handle that is strong and unbreakable,
for God hears all and knows every thing.
257. God is the friend of those who believe,
and leads them out of darkness into light;
but the patrons of infidels are idols and devils
who lead them from light into darkness.
They are the residents of Hell,
and will there for ever abide.

Have you thought of the man who argued
with Abraham about his Lord because
God had given him a kingdom? When Abraham said:
"My Lord is the giver of life and death," he replied:
"I am the giver of life and death."
And Abraham said: "God makes the sun rise from the East;
so you make it rise from the West,"
and dumbfounded was the infidel.
God does not guide those who are unjust.
259. Or take the man who passed by a town
which lay destroyed upside down. He said:
"How can God restore this city now that it is destroyed?"
So God made him die for a hundred years,
then brought him back to life, and inquired:
"How long did you stay in this state?"
"A day or less than a day," he replied.
"No," He said, "you were dead a hundred years,
yet look at your victuals, they have not decomposed;
and look at your ass!
We shall make you a warning for men.
And regard the bones, how We raise them
and clothe them with flesh."
When this became clear to him, the man said:
"Indeed God has power over all things."
260. Remember, when Abraham said: "O Lord,
show me how you raise the dead,"
He said: "What! Do you not believe?"
"I do," answered Abraham. "I only ask for my heart's
      assurance."
(The Lord) said: "Trap four birds and tame them,
then put each of them

24 THE LIGHT

which God has allowed to be raised,
and His name remembered in them.
His praises are sung there morning and evening,
37. By men not distracted from the remembrance of God
either by trade and commerce or buying and selling,
who stand by their devotional obligations
and pay the zakat, who fear the day
when hearts and eyes would flutter with trepidation
38. That God may reward them for the best of their deeds,
and bestow more on them of His bounty,
for God gives whom He please without measure.
39. As for those who disbelieve,
their deeds are like a mirage in the desert
which the thirsty takes for water
till he reaches it to find that there was nothing,
and finds God with him who settles his account,
for God is swift at the reckoning.
40. Or like darkness in a wide, wide sea,
waves surging upon waves, with clouds overhanging,
darkness on darkness.
If you stretch your hand, you could hardly see it.
For him whom God does not give
any light, there is no light.

Have you not seen that all those who are in the
        heavens and the earth,
and the birds on the wing, sing the praises of God.
Each one knows its obligations and its duties,
and God knows whatever they do.
42. For God's is the kingdom of the heavens and the earth,
and the returning is to God.
43. Have you not seen that God drives the clouds,
then joins them together and puts them fold on fold.
Then you see the rain fall through them;
and He sends down hail from the sky where there are
        mountains of it,
and strikes those with it with whom He will,
and wards it off from whomsoever He please.
His lightning could snatch away their eyes.
44. It is God who alternates night and day.
There is surely a lesson in this for men of sight.
45. God created every moving thing from water:
One crawls on its belly,
one walks on two legs, another moves on four.
God creates whatsoever He will.
Indeed God has power over every thing.

59 CONFRONTATION

٢٨ قد سمع الله   ٥٩ الحشر

where they will abide for ever.
This is the punishment for the wicked.

O you who believe, be fearful of God.
Let each soul consider
what it has sent (of good deeds) in advance for the morrow,
and fear God.
Surely God is aware of what you do.
19. And be not like those who have forgotten God,
so that God has made them forget themselves.
Such are the reprobates.
20. Alike are not the inmates of Hell
and the residents of Paradise.
The men of Paradise will be felicitous.
21. If We had sent down this Qur'an to a mountain
you would have seen it turn desolate
and split into two for fear of God.
We offer these examples to men
that they may think and reflect.
22. He is God; there is no god but He,
the knower of the unknown and the known.
He is the benevolent, ever-merciful.
23. He is God; there is no god but He,
the King, the Holy, the Preserver,
Protector, Guardian, the Strong, the Powerful, Omnipotent.
Far too exalted is God
for what they associate with Him.
24. He is God, the Creator, the Maker, the Fashioner.
His are all the names beautiful.
Whatever is in the heavens and the earth
sings His praises.
He is all-mighty and all-wise.

93   Early Hours of Morning

Ad-Duhā: Makki

بِسْمِ اللهِ الرَّحْمٰنِ الرَّحِيْمِ ۝

In the name of Allah, most benevolent, ever-merciful.

I CALL TO witness
the early hours of morning,
2. And the night when dark and still,
3. Your Lord has neither left you,
nor despises you.
4. What is to come is better for you
than what has gone before;
5. For your Lord will certainly give you,
and you will be content.
6. Did He not find you an orphan
and take care of you?
7. Did He not find you perplexed,
and show you the way?
8. Did He not find you poor
and enrich you?
9. So do not oppress the orphan,
10. And do not drive
the beggar away,
11. And keep recounting the favours of your Lord.

وَالضُّحٰى ۝

وَالَّيْلِ اِذَا سَجٰى ۝

مَا وَدَّعَكَ رَبُّكَ وَمَا قَلٰى ۝

وَلَلْاٰخِرَةُ خَيْرٌ لَّكَ مِنَ الْاُوْلٰى ۝

وَلَسَوْفَ يُعْطِيْكَ رَبُّكَ فَتَرْضٰى ۝

اَلَمْ يَجِدْكَ يَتِيْمًا فَاٰوٰى ۝

وَوَجَدَكَ ضَآلًّا فَهَدٰى ۝

وَوَجَدَكَ عَآئِلًا فَاَغْنٰى ۝

فَاَمَّا الْيَتِيْمَ فَلَا تَقْهَرْ ۝

وَاَمَّا السَّآئِلَ فَلَا تَنْهَرْ ۝

وَاَمَّا بِنِعْمَةِ رَبِّكَ فَحَدِّثْ ۝

Appendix 2
Some Useful Addresses

1. PERIODICAL PUBLICATIONS

Encounter
Piazza S. Apollinaire, 49
00186 Rome, Italy

Focus on Christian-Muslim Relations
Islamic Foundation
223 London Road
Leicester, England

Islamochristiana
Pontifical Institute of Arabic and Islamic Studies
Piazza S. Appollinaire, 49
00186 Rome, Italy

The Muslim Journal
910 W. van Buren, Suite 2100
Chicago, IL 60607
(312) 243-7600

The Muslim World
Hartford Seminary
77 Sherman Street
Hartford, CT 06105
(860) 232-4451

Newsletter
Task Force on Christian-Muslim Relations
Hartford Seminary
77 Sherman Street
Hartford, CT 06105
(860) 232-4451

Newsletter
Center for the Study of Islam and Christian-Muslim Relations
Selly Oak Colleges
Birmingham B29 6LE
England

2. MUSLIM ORGANIZATIONS

American Muslim Mission
   7351 S. Stony Island Ave.
   Chicago, IL 60649
   (312) 643-0700

American Muslim Council
   1212 New York Ave., NW, Suite 525
   Washington, D.C. 20005
   (202) 789-2262

Canadian Council of Muslim Women
   100 McLevin Ave., Unit 204A
   Scarborough, Ontario M1B 2V5
   Canada
   (416) 293-7041

Council of Muslim Communities of Canada
   100 McLevin Ave., Unit 204A
   Scarborough, Ontario M1B 2V5
   Canada
   (416) 293-2099

Federation of Islamic Associations in the United States and Canada
   17514 Woodward
   Detroit, MI 48403
   (313) 849-2147

Institute of Islamic Information and Education
   4390 N. Elston Ave.
   Chicago, IL 60641
   (312) 777-7443

International Institute of Islamic Thought
   P.O. Box 669
   555 Grove Street
   Herndon, VA 22070
   (703) 471-1133

Iqra' International Education Foundation
   831 S. Lafallin
   Chicago, IL 60607
   (312) 226-5694

Islam-West Associates
   74 Whitehorn Crescent
   Willowdale, Ontario M2J 3B2
   Canada
   (416) 493-0547

Islamic Book Service
   10900 W. Washington Street
   Indianapolis, IN 46231
   (317) 839-8150

Islamic Center of Washington, D.C.
   2551 Massachusetts Ave., NW
   Washington, D.C. 20008
   (202) 332-8343

Islamic Society of North America
   Box 38
   Plainfield, IN 46169
   (317) 839-8157

Muslim World League Office of North America
   134 W. 26th Street, 11th Floor
   New York, NY 10001
   (212) 627-4033

3. CHRISTIAN ORGANIZATIONS

Americans for Middle East Understanding, Inc.
   475 Riverside Drive, Room 241
   New York, NY 10115
   (212) 870-2053

Canadian Center for Ecumenism
   2065 Sherbrooke Street
   Montreal, Quebec H3H 1G6
   (514) 937-9176

Canadian Conference of Catholic Bishops' Office for Ecumenical and Interreligious Affairs
   90 Parent Ave.
   Ottawa, Ontario K1N 7B1
   Canada
   (613) 241-9461

Center for the Study of Islam and Christian-Muslim Relations
   Selly Oak Colleges
   Birmingham B29 6LE
   England

Duncan Black Macdonald Center for the Study of Islam and Christian-Muslim Relations
   Hartford Seminary
   77 Sherman Street
   Hartford, CT 06105
   (860) 232-4451

Ecumenical Forum of Canada
11 Madison Ave.
Toronto, Ontario M5R 2S2
Canada
(416) 924-9351

National Office of Catholic Bishops Secretariat for Ecumenical and Religious
Affairs
3211 4th Street NE
Washington, D.C. 20017
(202) 541-3035

Presbyterian Church USA Ecumenical and Interfaith Office
100 Witherspoon Street
Louisville, KY 40202-1396
(502) 569-5000

Task Force on Christian-Muslim Relations
National Council of the Churches of Christ in the USA
Hartford Seminary
77 Sherman Street
Hartford, CT 06105
(860) 232-4451

4. INTERFAITH ORGANIZATIONS

British Council of Churches
Edinburgh House
2 Eaton Gate
London SW1W 9BL
England

Interfaith Network (UK)
5-7 Tavistock Place
London WC1H 9SS
England

Jewish-Muslim Ongoing Trialogue Group
Kennedy Institute
Georgetown University
Washington, D.C. 20007

The National Conference of Christians, Jews and Muslims
71 5th Ave.
New York, NY 10003
(212) 206-0006

World Conference on Religion and Peace U.S. Committee
777 United Nations Plaza, Suite 9A
New York, NY 10017
(212) 687-2163

World Interfaith Education Association (Ontario)
154 University Avenue, Suite 200
Toronto, Ontario M5H 2Z4
Canada
(416) 340-6630

5. AUDIO-VISUAL MATERIALS

American Institute for Islamic Affairs
School for International Service
4900 Massachusetts Ave. W.
Washington, D.C. 20016

Films for the Humanities and Sciences
P.O. Box 2053
Princeton, NJ 08543-2053
(800) 257-5126

Films for the Humanities and Sciences
P.O. Box 1051
Fort Erie, Ontario L2A 5N8
Canada

Notes

INTRODUCTION

1. For a demographic, socioeconomic, and sociopolitical survey of the Islamic world in 1985, see Byron L. Haines and Frank L. Cooley, eds., *Christians and Muslims Together—An Exploration by Presbyterians* (Philadelphia: The Geneva Press, 1987), pp. 43-65; also Charles Kimball, *Striving Together: A Way Forward in Christian-Muslim Relations* (Maryknoll, N.Y.: Orbis Books, 1991), pp. 7-8.

1. ISLAM: AN INTRODUCTION FOR CHRISTIANS

1. William Stoddart, *Sufism* (Wellingborough, UK: The Aquarian Press, 1982), p. 26.

2. See James A. Bill and John Alden Williams, "Shi'i Islam and Roman Catholicism: An Ecclesial and Political Analysis," in *The Vatican, Islam, and the Middle East,* ed. Kail C. Ellis (Syracuse, N.Y.: Syracuse University Press, 1987), p. 71.

3. Ibid., pp. 84-85.

4. Ibid., p. 85.

5. Titus Burckhardt, cited in Stoddart, *Sufism,* p. 45.

6. See Reynold A. Nicholson, *The Mystics of Islam* (London: Routledge and Kegan Paul, 1975), p. 69.

7. Jalaluddin Rumi, cited in Nicholson, *The Mystics of Islam,* pp. 69-70.

8. Nicholson, *The Mystics of Islam,* pp. 28-49.

9. Ibid., p. 117.

10. Ibid., pp. 60-61.

11. Ibid., pp. 29, 71.

12. Muhyi al-Din Ibn 'Arabi, cited in Stoddart, *Sufism,* p. 70.

13. *The Cloud of Unknowing* and *The Book of Privy Counselling,* trans. William Johnston (New York: Image Books, 1973), p. 56.

14. John Cassian, *Conferences,* trans. Colm Luibheid (New York: Paulist Press, 1985), pp. 132-40.

15. John Climacus, *The Ladder of Divine Ascent,* trans. Colm Luibheid (New York: Paulist Press, 1982), pp. 45-47.

16. Mircea Eliade, *Yoga: Immortality and Freedom* (Princeton: Princeton University Press, 1971), pp. 63-65.

17. *The Way of a Pilgrim,* trans. Helen Bacovin (Garden City, N.Y.: Image Books, 1978).

18. Ibn 'Ata' Allah, *Kitab al-Hikam,* trans. into English by Victor Danner as *The Book of Wisdom,* in Victor Danner and Wheeler Thackson, *The Book of Wisdom* and *Intimate Conversations* (New York: Paulist Press, 1978), pp. 47-150.

19. Peter J. Awn, "Sufism," in *The Encyclopedia of Religion,* ed. Mircea Eliade (New York: Macmillan, 1987), 13:119-20.

20. For references to the *Spiritual Exercises,* see *The Spiritual Exercises of St. Ignatius,* trans. Louis J. Puhl (Chicago: Loyola University Press, 1951). Hereafter all references to the *Spiritual Exercises* are indicated as *SE.*

21. *Letters of St. Ignatius of Loyola,* trans. William J. Young (Chicago: Loyola University Press, 1959), p. 22.

22. Karl Rahner, *The Dynamic Element in the Church* (Montreal: Palm Publishers, 1964), p. 153.

2. THE HISTORICAL BACKGROUND

1. Sydney Nettleton Fisher, *The Middle East: A History* (London: Routledge and Kegan Paul, 1971), pp. 14-17.

2. Edgar Alexander, "Oriental Christianity," in *Background of the Middle East,* ed. Ernst Jackh (Ithaca, N.Y.: Cornell University Press, 1952), p. 68; De Lacy O'Leary, *How Greek Science Passed to the Arabs* (London: Routledge and Kegan Paul, 1948), pp. 6-8, 36.

3. W. Montgomery Watt, *Islamic Revelation in the Modern World* (Edinburgh: Edinburgh University Press, 1969), pp. 94-95.

4. Alan Richardson, *Creeds in the Making* (London: SCM Press, 1961), pp. 61-62; W. Montgomery Watt, *Muslim-Christian Encounters* (London and New York: Routledge, 1991), p. 2; John B. Carman, *Majesty and Meekness: A Comparative Study of Contrast and Harmony in the Concept of God* (Grand Rapids, Mich.: William B. Eerdmans, 1994), pp. 296-99.

5. Robert M. Grant, *Religion and Politics at the Council of Nicaea* (Chicago: University of Chicago Press, 1973), p. 9; Carman, *Majesty and Meekness,* p. 299; Joseph Mitsuo Kitagawa, *The Christian Tradition beyond Its European Captivity* (Philadelphia: Trinity Press International, 1992), pp. 8-9.

6. Joseph F. Kelly, "Ecumenical Councils," in *The Modern Catholic Encyclopedia,* ed. Michael Glazier and Monica Hellwig (Collegeville, Minn.: The Liturgical Press, 1994), p. 265.

7. Ibid.

8. On Arianism, see the article by M. Simonetti in *Encyclopedia of the Early Church,* ed. Angelo Di Bernardino (New York: Oxford University Press, 1992), 1:76-78.

9. On Nestorianism, see ibid., 2:594.

10. On Monophysitism, see ibid., 1:569-70.

11. Mohamed Talbi, "Islam and Dialogue—Some Reflections on a Current Topic," in *Christianity through Non-Christian Eyes,* ed. Paul J. Griffiths (Maryknoll, N.Y.: Orbis Books, 1990), p. 84.

12. Benjamin Braude and Bernard Lewis, "Introduction," in *Christians and Jews in the Ottoman Empire,* ed. Benjamin Braude and Bernard Lewis (New York: Holmes and Meier, 1982), p. 2.

13. Christopher Dawson, *The Making of Europe* (London: Sheed and Ward, 1932), p. 107.

14. Richard Bell, *The Origin of Islam in Its Christian Environment* (London: Macmillan, 1926), p. 1.

15. Margaret Smith, *Studies in Early Mysticism in the Near and Middle East* (London: Sheldon Press, 1931), p. 108. See also Loofty Levonian, *Studies in the Relationship between Islam and Christianity* (London: George Allen and Unwin, 1940), p. 112; Geoffrey Parrinder, *Jesus in the Qu'ran* (London: Faber and Faber, 1965), pp. 162-65.

16. Marshall G. S. Hodgson, *The Venture of Islam* (Chicago: University of Chicago Press, 1974), 1:199.

17. Erich W. Bethmann, *Bridge to Islam* (London: George Allen and Unwin, 1953), pp. 84-85.

18. Francis E. Peters, "The Early Muslim Empires: Ummayads, Abbasids, Fatimids," in *Islam: The Religious and Political Life of a World Community*, ed. Marjorie Kelly (New York: Praeger, 1984), p. 75.

19. On Islamic law, see H. A. R. Gibb, *Mohammedanism*, 2d rev. ed. (London: Oxford University Press, 1980), pp. 60-72; Ignaz Goldziher, *Introduction to Islamic Theology and Law*, trans. Andras and Ruth Hamori (Princeton: Princeton University Press, 1981), pp. 31-66; M. Khadduri and H. Liebesney, eds., *Law in the Middle East* (Washington, D.C.: Middle East Institute, 1955).

20. Bernard Lewis, "Politics and War," in *The Legacy of Islam*, ed. Joseph Schacht and C. E. Bosworth (Oxford: Oxford University Press, 1979), p. 159; see also Peters, "The Early Muslim Empires," p. 73.

21. John L. Esposito, *The Islamic Threat: Myth or Reality?* (New York: Oxford University Press, 1992), p. 39. See also Hodgson, *The Venture of Islam*, 1:199; Arthur Goldschmidt Jr., "The Colonial Period," in Kelly, *Islam*, p. 137.

22. Majid Khadduri, *War and Peace in the Law of Islam* (Baltimore: Johns Hopkins Press, 1955).

23. Cited by W. Wilson Cash, *Christendom and Islam: Their Contacts and Cultures down the Centuries* (London: SCM Press, 1937), pp. 48-49. See also Levonian, *Studies in the Relationship between Islam and Christianity*, p. 115; and T. W. Arnold, *The Preaching of Islam* (New York: Scribner's, 1913), p. 56.

24. Cash, *Christendom and Islam*, p. 104; J. H. Kramers, "Geography and Commerce," in *The Legacy of Islam*, ed. Thomas Arnold and Alfred Guillaume (Oxford: Clarendon Press, 1931), p. 81.

25. Edward Gibbon, *The Decline and Fall of the Roman Empire* (New York: Modern Library, n.d.), 3:56.

26. W. Montgomery Watt, *The Influence of Islam on Medieval Europe* (Edinburgh: Edinburgh University Press, 1972), p. 7.

27. Smith, *Studies in Early Mysticism in the Near and Middle East*, pp. 112-13; Cash, *Christendom and Islam*, pp. 71-72; Peters, "The Early Muslim Empires," pp. 80-81; James Kritzeck, *Sons of Abraham: Jews, Christians, and Moslems* (Baltimore and Dublin: Helicon, 1965), p. 61.

28. On the persecution of Christians by Muslims, see Peters, "The Early Muslim Empires," p. 79; Kritzek, *Sons of Abraham*, p. 49; Goldziher, *Introduction to Islamic Theology and Law*, pp. 33-36; Mohamed Talbi, "Religious Liberty: A Muslim Perspective," in *Religious Liberty and Human Rights in Nations and in*

Religions, ed. Leonard Swidler (Philadelphia: Ecumenical Press, 1986), pp. 175-87; Arnold, *The Preaching of Islam,* pp. 75-79 and 420-23; Levonian, *Studies in the Relationship between Islam and Christianity,* pp. 110-22; A. S. Tritton, *The Caliphs and Their Non-Muslim Subjects: A Critical Study of the Covenant of 'Umar* (London: Oxford University Press, 1930).

29. Arnold, *The Preaching of Islam,* p. 420.

30. Ibid.

31. Cited in Bethmann, *Bridge to Islam,* pp. 89-90. See also D. C. Monro, "The Speech of Urban II at Clermont, 1095," *American Historical Review* 11 (1905): 231-42.

32. Peters, "The Early Muslim Empires," p. 41. See also Karlfried Froehlich, "Crusades," in *The Encyclopedia of Religion,* ed. Mircea Eliade (New York: Macmillan, 1987), 4:168.

33. George Sarton, *Introduction to the History of Science* (Baltimore: Williams and Wilkins, 1927), 1:520-783; Richard Walzer, *Greek into Arabic: Essays on Islamic Philosophy* (Oxford: Bruno Cassirer, 1962), pp. 1-37.

34. Sarton, *Introduction to the History of Science,* pp. 167-480; Charles H. Haskins, *The Renaissance of the Twelfth Century* (Cambridge, Mass.: Harvard University Press, 1927).

35. Kritzeck, *Sons of Abraham,* p. 65.

36. Gustave E. von Grunebaum, *Medieval Islam: A Study in Cultural Orientation* (Chicago: University of Chicago Press, 1946), pp. 334-35.

37. Kritzeck, *Sons of Abraham,* p. 65; Etienne Gilson, *History of Christian Philosophy in the Middle Ages* (New York: Random House, 1955), pp. 179-225. For similarities between Al-Farabi's and Aquinas's arguments for the existence of God, God's attributes, and their theory of knowledge conveniently given in parallel columns, see Eugene A. Myers, *Arabic Thought and the Western World in the Golden Age of Islam* (New York: Frederick Ungar, 1964), pp. 17-30.

38. Miguel Asin y Palacios, *Islam and the Divine Comedy,* trans. Harold Sunderland (New York: E. P. Dutton, 1926); Myers, *Arabic Thought and the Western World in the Golden Age of Islam,* p. 51; Francesco Gabrieli, "Islam in the Mediterranean World," in Schacht and Bosworth, *The Legacy of Islam,* p. 94; Franz Rosenthal, "Literature," in Schacht and Bosworth, *The Legacy of Islam,* pp. 344-45.

39. Maxime Rodinson, "The Western Image and Western Studies of Islam," in Schacht and Bosworth, *The Legacy of Islam,* p. 91; Georges C. Anawati, "Philosophy, Theology, Mysticism," in Schacht and Bosworth, *The Legacy of Islam,* pp. 380-89; Kritzeck, *Sons of Abraham,* p. 66.

40. Watt, *The Influence of Islam on Medieval Europe,* p. 84.

41. Bethmann, *Bridge to Islam,* p. 93; Stephen Neill, *Crisis of Belief* (London: Hodder and Stoughton, 1984), pp. 59-60.

42. Erich W. Bethmann, *Steps toward Understanding Islam* (Washington, D.C.: American Friends of the Middle East, 1966), p. 47.

43. Ibid.

44. Ibid.

45. Arthur Goldschmidt Jr., *A Concise History of the Middle East,* 3d ed. (Boulder, Colo.: Westview Press, 1988), p. 132; Bernard Lewis, "Politics and War," in Schacht and Bosworth, *The Legacy of Islam,* pp. 200-201.

46. Byron Porter Smith, *Islam in English Literature,* edited with an introduction by S. B. Bushrui and Anahid Melikian and a foreword by Omar A. Farrukh

(Delmar, N.Y.: Caravan Books, 1977), pp. 16-17; Samuel Claggett Chew, *The Crescent and the Rose* (New York: Oxford University Press, 1937), pp. 101-2; Braude and Lewis, *Christians and Jews in the Ottoman Empire,* p. 3.

　47. Braude and Lewis, *Christians and Jews in the Ottoman Empire,* p. 1.

48. Fisher, *The Middle East,* p. 299.

49. Bethmann, *Steps toward Understanding Islam,* p. 48.

50. Maxime Rodinson, *Europe and the Mystique of Islam* (Seattle: University of Washington Press, 1987), p. 66.

51. Hugh Goddard, *Christians and Muslims: From Double Standards to Mutual Understanding* (Richmond, Surrey: Curzon Press, 1995), p. 136. See also Stephen Neill, *A History of Christian Missions* (Harmondsworth, Middlesex: Penguin Books, 1977), p. 259.

52. Braude and Lewis, *Christians and Jews in the Ottoman Empire,* pp. 29-32.

53. Kamel S. Abu Jaber, "The Millet System in the Nineteenth Century Ottoman Empire," *The Muslim World* 57/3 (1967): 221.

54. Ibid. See also A. H. Hourani, *Minorities in the Arab World* (London: Oxford University Press, 1947), pp. 23-24.

55. Bethmann, *Bridge to Islam,* p. 96.

56. Ibid.

57. John L. Esposito, *Islam and Politics* (Syracuse, N.Y.: Syracuse University Press, 1984), pp. 230-32.

58. E. I. J. Rosenthal, *Political Thought in Medieval Islam* (Cambridge: Cambridge University Press, 1968), p. 116.

59. Charles E. Curran, "Religious Freedom and Human Rights in the World and the Church: A Christian Perspective," in Swidler, *Religious Liberty and Human Rights in Nations and in Religions,* p. 145.

60. Ibid., p. 146.

61. Ibid., p. 150.

62. Ibid., p. 152.

63. Leonard Swidler, "Human Rights: A Historical Overview," in *The Ethics of the World Religions and Human Rights,* ed. Hans Küng and Jurgen Moltmann (London: SCM Press, 1990), pp. 20-21.

64. Kritzeck, *Sons of Abraham,* pp. 76-78; Wilfred Cantwell Smith, *Islam in Modern History* (Princeton: Princeton University Press, 1957), pp. 94-95.

65. On this issue see W. A. R. Shadid and P. S. Koningsveld, "Integration and Change," in *The Integration of Islam and Hinduism in Western Europe,* ed. W. A. R Shadid and P. S. Koningsveld (Kampen, The Netherlands: Kok Pharos Publishing House, 1991), pp. 228-30; Bernard Lewis, *Islam and the West* (New York and Oxford: Oxford University Press, 1993), pp. 43-57; Bernard Lewis, "Legal and Historical Reflections on the Position of Muslim Populations under Non-Muslim Rule," in *Muslims in Europe,* ed. Bernard Lewis and Dominique Schnapper (London: Pinter Publishers, 1994), pp. 1-18.

3. THEOLOGICAL ISSUES

1. See Norman Daniel, *Islam and the West: The Making of an Image* (Edinburgh: Edinburgh University Press, 1960), pp. 79-108.

2. Ibid. See also Byron Porter Smith, *Islam in English Literature,* edited with

an introduction by S. B. Bushrui and Anahid Melikian and a foreword by Omar A. Farrukh (Delmar, N.Y.: Caravan Books, 1977), pp. 1-19; Samuel Claggett Chew, *The Crescent and the Rose* (New York: Oxford University Press, 1937), pp. 387-451; Richard William Southern, *Western Views of Islam in the Middle Ages* (Cambridge, Mass.: Harvard University Press, 1962).

3. Chew, *The Crescent and the Rose*, p. 402.

4. Dante, *The Divine Comedy,* vol. 1: *Hell,* trans. Dorothy L. Sayers (Harmondsworth, Middlesex: Penguin Books, 1949), Canto 28:22-27.

5. James Kritzeck, *Peter the Venerable and Islam* (Princeton: Princeton University Press, 1964), pp. vii-viii.

6. W. Montgomery Watt, *Muslim-Christian Encounters* (London and New York: Routledge, 1991), p. 111.

7. Chew, *The Crescent and the Rose*, p. 449.

8. Ibid., p. 451.

9. "Ramon Lull," in *The Encyclopedia of Religion,* ed. Mircea Eliade (New York: Macmillan, 1987), 9:52.

10. James Thayer Addison, *The Christian Approach to the Moslem* (New York: Columbia University Press, 1942), p. 39.

11. Ibid., p. 40.

12. Jean-Marie Gaudeul, *Encounters and Clashes: Islam and Christianity in History* (Rome: Pontificio Istituto di Studi Arabi e Islamici, 1990), 1:191-92.

13. Ibid., p. 193.

14. Ibid., pp. 195-97.

15. Donald F. Duclow, "Nicholas of Cusa," in *The Encyclopedia of Religion,* ed. Mircea Eliade (New York: Macmillan, 1987), 10:431.

16. Alexander Ross, quoted by T. W. Arnold, *The Preaching of Islam* (New York: Scribner's, 1913), pp. 170-71.

17. Anne Freemantle, *Desert Calling: The Life of Charles de Foucald* (London: Hollis and Carter, 1950).

18. See the second prayer of Abraham in "The Three Prayers of Abraham," in Herbert Mason, ed., *Testimonies and Reflections: Essays of Louis Massignon* (Notre Dame, Ind.: University of Notre Dame Press, 1989), pp. 12-15; also Robert Caspar, "La vision de l'Islam chez Louiぅ Massignon et son influence sur l'Eglise," in *Louis Massignon,* ed. J.-F. Six (Paris: L'Herne, 1970), pp. 126-47.

19. Jean Mohammed Abd-el-Jalil, *Aspects intérieurs de l'Islam* (Paris: Seuil, 1949); Charles-J. Ledit, *Mahomet, Israel et le Christ* (Paris: La Colombe, 1956); Youakim Moubarac, *Abraham dans le Coran* (Paris: J. Vrin, 1958); Giulio Basetti-Sani, *Louis Massignon (1883-1962): Christian Ecumenist,* ed. and trans. Allan Harris Cutler (Chicago: Franciscan Herald Press, 1974); Herbert Mason, *Memoir of a Friend: Louis Massignon* (Notre Dame, Ind.: University of Notre Dame Press, 1988).

20. Yehezkel Landau, "Epilogue," in *Voices from Jerusalem,* ed. David Burrell and Yehezkel Landau (New York: Paulist Press, 1992), pp. 159-68.

21. Daniel J. Sahas, *John of Damascus on Islam* (Leiden: E. J. Brill, 1972), p. 133; Adel-Théodore Khoury, *Les théologiens Byzantines et l'Islam* (Louvain: Nauwelaerts, 1969).

22. Karl-Josef Kuschel, *Abraham: Sign of Hope for Jews, Christians, and Muslims* (New York: Continuum, 1995), pp. 86-87.

23. For example, René Daghorn, *La geste d'Ismael d'après l'onomastique et la tradition arabes* (Geneva: Droz, 1981).

24. Kuschel, *Abraham*, pp. 158-64.

25. Gregory VII, cited by Norman Daniel, *The Arabs and Medieval Europe* (London: Longman, 1975), pp. 250-51. See also Thomas Michel, "Christian-Muslim Dialogue in a Changing World," *Theology Digest* 39/4 (1992): 305.

26. Neal Robinson, "Massignon, Vatican II, and Islam as an Abrahamic Religion," *Islam and Christian-Muslim Relations* 2/2 (1991): 196.

27. Karl Rahner, "Christianity and Non-Christian Religions," in *Theological Investigations* (Baltimore: Helicon Press, 1966; London: Darton, Longman, and Todd, 1966), 5:115-34; see also idem, *Foundations of Christian Faith* (New York: Seabury Press, 1978), pp. 138-75.

28. René Latourelle, *Theology of Revelation* (Staten Island: Alba House, 1987); Gabriel Moran, *Theology of Revelation* (New York: Herder and Herder, 1966); idem, *The Present Revelation* (New York: Herder and Herder, 1972); Aylward Shorter, *Revelation and Its Interpretation* (London: G. Chapman, 1983); Avery Dulles, *Models of Revelation* (Garden City, N.Y.: Doubleday, 1983); idem, "Faith and Revelation," in *Systematic Theology: Roman Catholic Perspectives,* ed. Francis Schüssler Fiorenza and John P. Gavin (Dublin: Gill and Macmillan, 1992), pp. 91-128.

29. Richard P. McBrien, *Catholicism* (New York: HarperCollins, 1994), p. 252.

30. Jacques Dupuis, *Jesus Christ at the Encounter of World Religions* (Maryknoll, N.Y.: Orbis Books, 1991), pp. 170-71.

31. Stuart E. Brown, trans., *The Challenge of the Scriptures: The Bible and the Qur'an* (Maryknoll, N.Y.: Orbis Books, 1989), p. 66.

32. Ibid., p. 62.

33. Ibid., p. 63, citing *Summa Theologica,* IIa-IIae, q.1, art. 2, ad. 2. See also Gregory Baum, *Man Becoming* (New York: Herder and Herder, 1970), p. 8.

34. The shift in the understanding of truth complements the shift in the understanding of revelation. On this point see Leonard Swidler, "Interreligious and Interideological Dialogue: The Matrix for All Systematic Reflection Today," in *Toward a Universal Theology of Religion,* ed. Leonard Swidler (Maryknoll, N.Y.: Orbis Books, 1988), pp. 7-13.

35. David A. Kerr, "Prophethood," in *The Oxford Encyclopedia of the Modern Islamic World,* ed. John L. Esposito (New York: Oxford University Press, 1995), 3:365; Amina Wadud-Mushin, "Revelation," in ibid., 3:430; A. J. Arberry, *Reason and Revelation in Islam* (London: George Allen and Unwin, 1965), pp. 12-15.

36. Fazlur Rahman, "Christian Particularity and the Faith of Islam," in *Christian Faith in a Religiously Plural World,* ed. Donald G. Dawe and John B. Carman (Maryknoll, N.Y.: Orbis Books, 1978), p. 71.

37. Mahmoud Ayoub, "The Word of God in Islam," in *Orthodox Christians and Muslims,* ed. N. M. Vaporis (Brookline, Mass.: Holy Cross Orthodox Press, 1986), p. 77.

38. Mohamed Talbi, "Islam and Dialogue—Some Reflections on a Current Topic," in *Christianity and Islam: The Struggling Dialogue,* ed. Richard W. Rousseau (Montrose, Pa.: Ridge Row Press, 1985), pp. 70-71.

39. Ayoub, "The Word of God in Islam," p. 74.

40. Mahmoud Ayoub, "Qur'an," in *The Oxford Encyclopedia of the Modern Islamic World,* ed. John L. Esposito (New York: Oxford University Press, 1995), 3:385.

41. Ayoub, "The Word of God in Islam," p. 74.

42. Ibid.

43. Rahman, "Christian Particularity and the Faith of Islam," p. 78.

44. On the role of the Holy Spirit in the world religions, see Frederick E. Crowe, "Son of God, Holy Spirit, and World Religions," in *Appropriating the Lonergan Idea*, ed. Michael Vertin (Washington, D.C.: Catholic University of America Press, 1989), pp. 324-43; Georges Khodr, "The Economy of the Holy Spirit," in *Mission Trends No. 5: Faith Meets Faith*, ed. Gerald H. Anderson and Thomas F. Stransky (New York: Paulist Press, 1981), pp. 36-49.

45. Bert F. Breiner, "Islam, Language, and Law: A Response," in *Ecumenism* 116 (December 1994): 19.

46. Thomas Michel, "Islamo-Christian Dialogue: Reflections on the Recent Teachings of the Church," Secretariatus pro Non-Christianis, *Bulletin* 20/2 (1985): 183.

47. John Paul II, *Origins* 9/26 (1979): 419.

48. Ibid. 10/37 (1981): 592.

49. John Paul II, cited by Michel, "Islamo-Christian Dialogue," p. 184.

50. Mahmoud Ayoub, "The Traditional Western Analysis: A Response," *Ecumenism* 116 (December 1994): 16.

51. Dupuis, *Jesus Christ at the Encounter of World Religions*, p. 124; see also Michel, "Islamo-Christian Dialogue, p. 184.

52. Dupuis, *Jesus Christ at the Encounter of World Religions*, p. 124.

53. Jan van Lin, "Mission and Dialogue: God and Jesus Christ," in *Muslims and Christians in Europe Breaking New Ground: Essays in Honor of Jan Slomp*, ed. Gé Speelman, Jan van Lin, and Dick Mulder (Kampen, The Netherlands: Uitgeverij Kok, 1993), pp. 153, 167.

54. Sydney H. Griffith, "The Gospel in Arabic: An Inquiry into Its Appearance in the First Abbasid Century," *Oriens Christianus* 69 (1985): 126-67.

55. Khalifa Abdul Hakim, cited in Erich W. Bethmann, *Steps toward Understanding Islam* (Washington, D.C.: American Friends of the Middle East, 1966), p. 18. See also Isma'il R. Al Faruqi, "Islamic Ethics," in *World Religions and Global Ethics*, ed. S. Cromwell Crawford (New York: Paragon House, 1989), pp. 215, 218-19.

56. See, for example, M. Kamel Husayn's account of the crucifixion from a Muslim perspective in his *City of Wrong*, trans. Kenneth Cragg (Amsterdam: Djambatan, 1959).

57. F. R. Tennant, *The Sources of the Doctrines of the Fall and Original Sin* (New York: Schocken Books, 1968), pp. 275-96, 325-28; Henri Rondet, *Original Sin: The Patristic and Theological Background* (Shannon, Ireland: Ecclesia Press, 1972), pp. 25-132.

58. John Hick, *Evil and the God of Love* (San Francisco: Harper & Row, 1978), p. 212.

59. For example, Piet Schoonenberg, *Man and Sin* (London: Sheed and Ward, 1965), pp. 98-191; Peter de Rosa, *Christ and Original Sin* (Milwaukee: Bruce, 1967), pp. 73-134; Langdon Gilkey, *Message and Existence* (San Francisco: Harper & Row, 1978), pp. 117-57.

60. Rahner, *Foundations of Christian Faith*, pp. 106-15.

61. See Gerald O'Collins, "Doctrine of Atonement," in *The HarperCollins Encyclopedia of Catholicism*, ed. Richard P. McBrien (New York: HarperCollins, 1995), p. 110; Richard P. McBrien, *Catholicism* (New York: HarperCollins, 1994), pp. 444-45; Alan Richardson, *Creeds in the Making* (London: SCM Press, 1961),

pp. 108-10; Robin Boyd, *Khristadvaita* (Madras: The Christian Literature Society, 1977), pp. 189-94.

62. Khodr, "The Economy of the Holy Spirit," p. 45.

63. Alphonse Mingana, "The Apology of Timothy the Patriarch before the Caliph Mahdi," *Bulletin of the John Rylands Library* 12 (1928): 197.

64. Cardinal Tarancon, cited in Emilio G. Aguilar, "The Second International Muslim-Christian Congress of Cordoba (March 21-27, 1977)," in Rousseau, *Christianity and Islam*, p. 165.

65. R. C. Zaehner, *At Sundry Times: An Essay in the Comparison of Religions* (London: Faber and Faber, 1958), pp. 27, 153-55; Charles-J. Ledit, *Mahomet, Israel et le Christ*; Louis Massignon, "Le Signe Marial," *Rythmes du Monde* 3 (1948): 7-16; Michael Hayek, *Le Mystère d'Ismael* (Paris: Maison Mame, 1964); Hans Küng, "Christianity and World Religions: Dialogue with Islam," in Swidler, *Toward a Universal Theology of Religion*, pp. 196-98; Claude Geffré, "Le Coran, une parole de Dieu différente?" *Lumière et Vie* 32 (1983): 21-32; Robert Caspar, "La rencontre des théologies," *Lumière et Vie* 32 (1983): 63-68; Michael Lelong, "Mahomet, prophète de l'Islam," *Studia Missionalia* 33 (1984): 251-76.

66. Kenneth Cragg, *Muhammed and the Christian* (Maryknoll, N.Y.: Orbis Books, 1984), pp. 92-93; R. H. Drummond, "Towards a Theological Understanding of Islam," *Journal of Ecumenical Studies* 9/4 (1972): 777-801; W. Montgomery Watt, *Islam and Christianity Today* (London: Routledge and Kegan Paul, 1983), pp. 60-61. For an analysis of the reasons for considering Muhammad a prophet in the thought of Massignon, Ledit, Hayek, Küng, Cragg, and Watt, see David A. Kerr, "'He Walked in the Path of the Prophets': Toward Christian Theological Recognition of the Prophethood of Muhammad," in *Christian-Muslim Encounters*, ed. Yvonne Yazbeck Haddad and Wadi Zaidan Haddad (Gainesville, Fla.: University Press of Florida, 1995), pp. 426-46.

67. Dupuis, *Jesus Christ at the Encounter of World Religions*, p. 174; Brown, *The Challenge of the Scriptures*, p. 61.

68. Karl Rahner, "Toward a Fundamental Theological Interpretation of Vatican II," *Theological Studies* 40:4 (1979): 717.

69. See Leonard Swidler, *The Meaning of Life at the Edge of the Third Millennium* (New York: Paulist Press, 1992), pp. 98-102; John Hick, ed., *The Myth of God Incarnate* (London: SCM Press, 1977).

70. Karl Rahner, "Remarks on the Dogmatic Treatise '*De Trinitate*,'" in *Theological Investigations* (Baltimore: Helicon Press, 1966), 4:79.

4. FACING THE FUTURE

1. Mohamed Talbi, "Islam and Dialogue—Some Reflections on a Current Topic," in *Christianity and Islam: The Struggling Dialogue*, ed. Richard W. Rousseau (Montrose, Pa.: Ridge Row Press, 1985), p. 62.

2. Ibid., p. 61.

3. Khalid Duran, "Muslims and Non-Muslims," in *Muslims in Dialogue*, ed. Leonard Swidler (Lewiston, N.Y.: Edwin Mellen Press, 1992), p. 102.

4. Riffat Hassan, "On Human Rights and the Qur'anic Perspective," in Swidler, *Muslims in Dialogue*, p. 457.

5. Syed Z. Abedin, "Believers and the Promotion of Mutual Trust," in Munawar Ahmad Anees, Syed Z. Abedin, and Ziauddin Sardar, *Christian-Muslim Relations Yesterday, Today, Tomorrow* (London: Grey Seal, 1991), p. 48.

6. Khurshid Ahmad, "Christian Mission and Islamic *Da'wah*," in World Council of Churches, *Meeting in Faith: Twenty Years of Christian-Muslim Conversations Sponsored by the World Council of Churches*, comp. Stuart E. Brown (Geneva: WCC, 1989), pp. 75-78.

7. Ibid., p. 75.

8. Ibid., p. 76.

9. See the following in Swidler, *Muslims in Dialogue:* Hasan Askari, "The Dialogical Relationship between Christianity and Islam," pp. 37-48; Khalid Duran, "Interreligious Dialogue and the Islamic 'Original Sin,'" pp. 49-58; Abdullahi Ahmed An-Na'im, "Mahmud Muhammad Taha and the Crisis in Islamic Law Reform: Implications for Interreligious Relations," pp. 59-85; and Mohamed Talbi, "Possibilities and Conditions for a Better Understanding between Islam and the West," pp. 111-53.

10. Talbi, "Islam and Dialogue," p. 58.

11. Ibid., p. 59.

12. For Muslim scholarship see Anees, Abedin, and Sardar, *Christian-Muslim Relations Yesterday, Today, Tomorrow*; Muhammad Mushuq ibn Ally, "Theology of Islamic Liberation," in *World Religions and Human Liberation*, ed. Dan Cohn-Sherbok (Maryknoll, N.Y.: Orbis Books, 1992), pp. 44-62; Seyyed Nasr, "Islam and the Environmental Crisis," in *Spirit and Nature: Why the Environment Is a Religious Issue*, ed. Steven C. Rockfeller and John C. Elder (Boston: Beacon Press, 1992), pp. 83-108; Asghar Ali Engineer, *Islam and Liberation Theology* (New Delhi: Sterling Publishers, 1990).

For Christian scholarship see Hans Küng, *Global Responsibility: In Search of a New World Ethic* (New York: Crossroad, 1991); Hans Küng and Karl-Josef Kuschel, eds., *A Global Ethic: The Declaration of the Parliament of the World's Religions* (New York: Continuum, 1993); Paul Knitter, *One Earth Many Religions* (Maryknoll, N.Y.: Orbis Books, 1995); idem, "Toward a Liberation Theology of Religions," in *The Myth of Christian Uniqueness*, ed. John Hick and Paul F. Knitter (Maryknoll, N.Y.: Orbis Books, 1987), pp. 178-200.

13. Ziauddin Sardar, "The Postmodern Age," in Anees, Abedin, and Sardar, *Christian-Muslim Relations Yesterday, Today, Tomorrow*, p. 82.

14. Abedin, "Believers and the Promotion of Mutual Trust," p. 40.

15. Ibid.

16. John Paul II, *Origins* 13/9 (1979): 419-20.

17. Sardar, "The Postmodern Age," p. 84.

18. On the Program for Dialogue with People of Living Faiths and Ideologies, see Konrad Raiser, *Ecumenism in Transition: A Paradigm Shift in the Ecumenical Movement?* (Geneva: World Council of Churches, 1991), pp. 54-55.

19. World Council of Churches, *Guidelines on Dialogue with People of Living Faiths and Ideologies* (Geneva: World Council of Churches, 1979).

20. Raiser, *Ecumenism in Transition*, p. 55.

21. Wesley Ariarajah, *The Bible and People of Other Faiths* (Geneva: World Council of Churches, 1985), pp. 58ff.; Stanley Samartha, *Courage for Dialogue: Ecumenical Issues in Interreligious Relationships* (Geneva: World Council of

Churches, 1981), pp. 49ff.; José Míguez Bonino, "The Concern for a Vital and Coherent Theology," *Ecumenical Review* 41/2 (1989): 160-76.

22. Raiser, *Ecumenism in Transition,* p. 58.

23. John Hick, "Trinity and Incarnation in the Light of Religious Pluralism," in *Three Faiths—One God,* ed. John Hick and Edmund S. Meltzer (Albany, N.Y.: State University of New York Press, 1989), p. 199.

24. Ibid., p. 200.

25. Ibid., p. 201.

26. Ibid.

27. Muzammil H. Siddiqi, "A Muslin Response to John Hick: Trinity and Incarnation in the Light of Religious Pluralism," in Hick and Meltzer, *Three Faiths—One God,* pp. 211-13.

28. See World Council of Churches, *Meeting in Faith,* pp. 21-29 and 119-32.

29. Charles Kimball, *Striving Together: A Way Forward in Christian-Muslim Relations* (Maryknoll, N.Y.: Orbis Books, 1991), pp. 92-93.

30. For accounts of these meetings, see World Council of Churches, *Meeting in Faith,* pp. 133-81.

31. Kimball, *Striving Together,* p. 95.

32. John Paul II, cited in Jan van Lin, "Mission and Dialogue: God and Jesus Christ," in *Muslims and Christians in Europe Breaking New Ground,* ed. Gé Speelman, Jan van Lin, and Dick Mulder (Kampen, The Netherlands: Uitgeverij Kok, 1993), pp. 164 and 167.

33. Jacques Dupuis, *Jesus Christ at the Encounter of World Religions,* trans. Robert R. Barr (Maryknoll, N.Y.: Orbis Books, 1991), p. 124.

34. Maurice Borrmans, *Guidelines for Dialogue between Christians and Muslims* (New York: Paulist Press, 1990), pp. 10-11.

35. Pontifical Council for Interreligious Dialogue and Congregation for the Evangelization of Peoples, *Dialogue and Proclamation,* no. 42; also *Redemptoris Missio,* no. 57. Both documents can be found in William R. Burrows, ed., *Redemption and Dialogue* (Maryknoll, N.Y.: Orbis Books, 1993).

36. See John Paul II, *Recognize the Spiritual Bonds Which Unite Us: Sixteen Years of Christian-Muslim Dialogue* (Vatican City: Pontifical Council for Interreligious Dialogue, 1994).

37. "The Pope's Message to Young Muslims," in Secretariatus pro Non-Christianis, *Bulletin* 20/3 (1985): 249-57.

38. See *Origins* 20/41 (1991): 671-72.

39. See John Borelli, "The Goals and Fruit of Catholic-Muslim Dialogue," *The Living Light* 32/2 (1995): 57.

40. Francis Arinze, "The Way Ahead for Muslims and Christians," Pontificium Consilium pro Dialogo inter Religiones, *Pro Dialogo Bulletin* 91/1 (1996): 26-32.

41. Ibid., p. 27.

42. *The Catholic New Times* [Toronto] 21/6 (30 March 1997), p. 2.

43. For a description of local situations of dialogue, see *Islamochristiana:* Michael L. Fitzgerald, "Christian-Muslim Dialogue in South-East Asia," no. 2 (1976): 171-85; Ali Merad, "Rapports de l'Eglise avec les Musulmans d'Europe," no. 3 (1977): 197-205; Michel Lelong, "Le Secrétariat de l'Eglise de France pour les Relations avec l'Islam," no. 4 (1978):165-74; Christian W. Troll, "Christian-

Muslim Relations in India, A Critical Survey," no. 5 (1979): 119-45; Michel Lagarde, "Quelques aspects concrete du dialogue islamo-chrétien au Mali," no. 5 (1979): 147-70; Joseph Kenny, "Christian-Muslim Relations in Nigeria," no. 5 (1979): 171-92; Penelope Johnstone, "Christians and Muslims in Britain," no. 7 (1981): 167-99 and no. 12 (1986): 181-90; R. Marston Speight, "Christian-Muslim Dialogue in the United States of America," no. 7 (1981): 201-210; Peter G. Gowing, "Christian-Muslim Dialogue in the Philippines, 1976-1981," no. 7 (1981): 211-25; Laurence P. Fitzgerald, "Christians and Muslims in Australia," no. 10 (1984): 159-76; Gerrie Lubbe, "Muslims and Christians in South Africa," no. 13 (1987): 113-29; Achilles de Souza, "Dialogue in the Islamic Republic of Pakistan," no. 14 (1988): 211-18; Piet Reesink, "Chrétiens et Musulmans au Pays Bas," no. 14 (1988): 237-53; Heinze Klautke, "Muslim and Christian Relations in West Germany," no. 14 (1988): 255-66; Peter Smith, "Christianity and Islam in Tanzania," no. 16 (1990): 171-82; Jean Landousies, "Chrétiens et Musulmans en Algérie," no. 17 (1991): 99-129; Henri Coudray, "Chrétiens et Musulmans au Tchad," no. 18 (1992): 175-234; Paul Tan Chee Ing, "Muslim-Christian Relations in Malaysia," no. 19 (1993): 125-51; Patrick D. Gaffrey, "Christian-Muslim Relations in Uganda," no. 20 (1994): 131-77; Sebastiano D'Ambra, "Christian-Muslim Relations in the Philippines," no. 20 (1994): 179-206. See also Abdullahi Ahmed An-Na'im, "Christian-Muslim Relations in the Sudan," in *The Vatican, Islam, and the Middle East,* ed. Kail C. Ellis (Syracuse, N.Y.: Syracuse University Press, 1987), pp. 265-76.

44. Paul Varo Martinson, ed., *Islam: An Introduction for Christians* (Minneapolis: Augsburg, 1994), pp. 74-76; Speight, "Christian-Muslim Dialogue in the United States of America," p. 202.

45. Aminah Beverly McCloud, *African American Islam* (New York and London: Routledge, 1955). R. Marston Speight, *Christian-Muslim Relations: An Introduction for Christians in the United States of America* (Hartford, Conn.: Task Force on Christian-Muslim Relations, National Council of Churches of Christ in the USA, 1983), pp. 37-38; Martinson, *Islam,* pp. 76-81.

46. The Women's Committee of the Muslim Students Association, *Parents' Manual: A Guide for Muslim Parents Living in North America* (Brentwood, Md.: American Trust Publications, 1976), p. 21.

47. See Yvonne Yazbeck Haddad, "Muslims in the United States," in *Islam: The Religious and Political Life of a World Community,* ed. Marjorie Kelly (New York: Praeger, 1984), pp. 259-74; Yvonne Yazbeck Haddad and Adair T. Lummis, *Islamic Values in the United States* (New York: Oxford University Press, 1987); Yvonne Yazbeck Haddad and Jane Idleman Smith, eds., *Muslim Communities in North America* (Albany, N.Y.: State University of New York Press, 1994); Akbar Muhammad, "Muslim Relations in the United States," in Seyd Z. Abedin and Ziauddin Sardar, eds., *Muslim Minorities in the West* (London: Grey Seal, 1995), pp. 159-77; Theodore Pulcini, "Values Conflict among U.S. Muslim Youth," in ibid., pp. 178-203; Sulayman S. Nyang, "Challenges Facing Christian-Muslim Dialogue in the United States," in Yvonne Yazbeck Haddad and Wadi Zaidan Haddad, eds., *Christian-Muslim Encounters* (Gainesville, Fla.: University Press of Florida, 1995), pp. 328-41.

48. See Baha Abu Jaban, "The Muslim Community in Canada," in Abedin and Sardar, *Muslim Minorities in the West,* pp. 134-49; Yvonne Y. Haddad, "Muslims in Canada," in *Religion and Ethnicity,* ed. Harold Coward and Leslie Kawamura

(Waterloo, Ont.: Wilfrid Laurier University Press, 1978), pp. 71-100; Zohra Husaini, *Muslims in the Canadian Mosaic: Socio-Cultural and Economic Links with Their Countries of Origin* (Edmonton, Alberta: Muslim Research Foundation, 1990); Earle H. Waugh, "North America and the Adaptation of the Muslim Tradition," in *Muslim Families in North America*, ed. Earle H. Waugh, Sharon McIrvin Abu Laban, and Regula Burckhardt Qureshi (Edmonton: The University of Alberta Press, 1991), pp. 80-87.

49. Martinson, *Islam*, pp. 103-6.

50. Ibid., p. 105.

51. Ibid., p. 104.

52. *Origins* 24/14 (1994): 250.

53. Hick and Meltzer, *Three Faiths—One God.*

54. George B. Grose and Benjamin J. Hubbard, eds., *The Abraham Connection: A Jew, Christian, and Muslim in Dialogue* (Notre Dame, Ind.: Cross Cultural Publications, 1994).

55. Swidler, *Muslims in Dialogue.*

56. Jorgen S. Nielsen, "Great Britain," in *The Oxford Encyclopedia of the Modern Islamic World*, ed. John L. Esposito (New York: Oxford University Press, 1995), 2:70.

57. Ibid.

58. M. Y. McDermott and M. M. Ahsan, *The Muslim Guide: For Teachers, Employers, Community Workers and Social Administrators in Britain* (Leicester: Islamic Foundation, 1980).

59. David Brown, *A New Threshold: Guidelines for the Churches in Their Relations with Muslim Communities* (London: BCC, 1976), p. 21.

60. Ibid., p. 23.

61. Penelope Johnstone, "Christians and Muslims in Britain," *Islamochristiana* 7 (1981): 187.

62. *Relations with People of Other Faiths: Guidelines on Dialogue in Britain* (London: BCC, 1981).

63. *Towards a Theology of Inter-Faith Dialogue*, 2d ed. (Toronto: Anglican Book Center, 1986).

64. Ibid., p. 27.

65. Ibid.

66. Johnstone, "Christians and Muslims in Britain," p. 191.

67. Ibid.

68. Ibid.

69. Jorgen S. Nielsen, "The Interfaith Network (UK) and Interfaith Relations," *Islam and Christian-Muslim Relations* 2/1 (1991): 107.

70. Akbar S. Ahmed, *Postmodernism and Islam: Predicament and Promise* (London and New York: Routledge, 1992), p. 176.

71. Seyyed Hossein Nasr, "On Being Muslim in the West," in *Muslim Wise*, 7 June 1990; cited by Ahmed, *Postmodernism and Islam: Predicament and Promise*, p. 158.

72. Shabbir Akhtar, *A Faith for All Seasons* (Chicago: Ivan R. Dee, 1990).

73. *Towards a Theology of Inter-Faith Dialogue*, p. 35.

74. *Relations with People of Other Faiths*, p. 7.

75. Kimball, *Striving Together*, p. 121.

Bibliography

Abbott, Walter M., ed. *The Documents of Vatican II*. New York: America Press, 1966.

Abd-el-Jalil, Jean Mohammed. *Aspects intérieurs de l'Islam*. Paris: Seuil, 1949.

Abedin, Seyd Z., and Ziauddin Sardar, eds. *Muslim Minorities in the West*. London: Grey Seal, 1995.

Abu Jaber, Kamel S. "The Millet System in the Nineteenth Century Ottoman Empire," *The Muslim World* 57/3 (1967): 212-23.

Addison, James Thayer. *The Christian Approach to the Moslem*. New York: Columbia University Press, 1942.

Ahmad, Khurshid. "Christian Mission and Islamic *Da'wah*." In World Council of Churches. *Meeting in Faith: Twenty Years of Christian-Muslim Conversations Sponsored by the World Council of Churches*. Compiled by Stuart E. Brown. Geneva: World Council of Churches, 1989.

Ahmed, Akbar S. *Postmodernism and Islam: Predicament and Promise*. London and New York: Routledge, 1992.

Akhtar, Shabbir. *A Faith for All Seasons: Islam and the Challenge of the Modern World*. Chicago: Ivan R. Dee, 1990.

Algabib, Hamid. "Letter to Pope John Paul II," *Origins* 20/41 (1991): 671-72.

Ali, Syed Ameer. *The Spirit of Islam*. London: Methuen, 1965.

Anderson, Gerald H., and Thomas F. Stransky, eds. *Mission Trends No. 5: Faith Meets Faith*. New York: Paulist Press, 1981.

Anees, Munawar Ahmad, Seyd Z. Abedin, and Ziauddin Sardar. *Christian-Muslim Relations Yesterday, Today, Tomorrow*. London: Grey Seal, 1991.

An-Na'im, Abdullahi Ahmed. "Christian-Muslim Relations in the Sudan: Peaceful Coexistence at Risk." In *The Vatican, Islam, and the Middle East*, edited by Kail C. Ellis. Syracuse, N.Y.: Syracuse University Press, 1987.

——————. "Mahmud Muhammad Taha and the Crisis in Islamic Law Reform: Implications for Interreligious Relations." In *Muslims in Dialogue*, edited by Leonard Swidler. Lewiston, N.Y.: Edwin Mellen Press, 1992.

Arberry, A. J. *Reason and Revelation in Islam*. London: George Allen and Unwin, 1965.

——————. *Sufism*. New York: Harper & Row, 1970.

Ariarajah, Wesley. *The Bible and People of Other Faiths*. Geneva: World Council of Churches, 1985.

Arinze, Francis. "The Way Ahead for Muslims and Christians." Pontificium Consilium pro Dialogo inter Religiones. *Pro Dialogo Bulletin* 91/1 (1996): 26-32.

Arnold, T. W. *The Preaching of Islam*. New York: Scribner's, 1913.

Arnold, T. W., and Alfred Guillaume, eds. *The Legacy of Islam*. Oxford: Clarendon Press, 1931. Republished 1974.

Asin y Palacios, Miguel. *Islam and the Divine Comedy.* Translated by Harold Sunderland. New York: E. P. Dutton, 1926.

Askari, Hasan. "The Dialogical Relationship between Christianity and Islam." In *Muslims in Dialogue*, edited by Leonard Swidler. Lewiston, N.Y.: Edwin Mellen Press, 1992.

Awn, Peter J. "Sufism." In *The Encyclopedia of Religion*, edited by Mircea Eliade. Vol. 13. New York: Macmillan, 1987.

Ayoub, Mahmoud. *Redemptive Suffering in Islam: A Study of the Devotional Aspects of 'Ashura' in Twelver Shi'ism.* Mouton: The Hague, 1978.

——————. "The Traditional Western Analysis: A Response." *Ecumenism* 116 (December 1994): 16-17.

——————. "The Word of God in Islam." In *Orthodox Christians and Muslims*, edited by N. M. Vaporis. Brookline, Mass.: Holy Cross Orthodox Press, 1986.

Basetti-Sani, Giulio. *Louis Massignon (1883-1962): Christian Ecumenist.* Edited and translated by Allan Harris Cutler. Chicago: Franciscan Herald Press, 1974.

Baum, Gregory. *Man Becoming.* New York: Herder and Herder, 1970.

Bell, Richard. *The Origin of Islam in Its Christian Environment.* London: Macmillan, 1926.

Bethmann, Erich W. *Bridge to Islam.* London: George Allen and Unwin, 1953.

——————. *Steps toward Understanding Islam.* Washington, D.C.: American Friends of the Middle East, 1966.

Bill, James A., and John Alden Williams. "Shi'i Islam and Roman Catholicism: An Ecclesial and Political Analysis." In *The Vatican, Islam, and the Middle East*, edited by Kail C. Ellis. Syracuse, N.Y.: Syracuse University Press, 1987.

Borelli, John. "The Goals and Fruit of Catholic-Muslim Dialogue." *The Living Light* 32:2 (1995): 51-60.

Borrmans, Maurice. *Guidelines for Dialogue between Christians and Muslims.* New York: Paulist Press, 1990.

Boyd, Robin. *Khristadvaita.* Madras: The Christian Literature Society, 1977.

Braude, Benjamin, and Bernard Lewis, eds. *Christians and Jews in the Ottoman Empire: The Functioning of a Plural Society.* New York: Holmes and Meier, 1982.

Breiner, Bert F. "Islam, Language, and Law: A Response." *Ecumenism* 116 (December 1994): 18-20.

Brown, Stuart E., trans. *The Challenge of the Scriptures: The Bible and the Qur'an.* Maryknoll, N.Y.: Orbis Books, 1989.

Bruce, F. F., and E. G. Rupp, eds. *Holy Book and Holy Tradition.* Manchester: Manchester University Press, 1968.

Burrell, David, and Yehezkel Landau, eds. *Voices from Jerusalem.* New York: Paulist Press, 1992.

Burrows, William R., ed. *Redemption and Dialogue: Reading "Redemptoris Missio" and "Dialogue and Proclamation."* Maryknoll, N.Y.: Orbis Books, 1993.

Carman, John B. *Majesty and Meekness: A Comparative Study of Contrast and Harmony in the Concept of God.* Grand Rapids, Mich.: William B. Eerdmans, 1994.

Cash, W. Wilson. *Christendom and Islam: Their Contacts and Cultures Down the Centuries*. London: SCM Press, 1937.

Caspar, Robert. "The Religious Value of Moslem Faith." Secretariatus pro Non-Christianis. *Bulletin* 13 (1970): 25-37.

——. "La rencontre des théologies." *Lumière et Vie* 32 (1983): 63-68.

——. "La vision de l'Islam chez Louis Massignon et son influence sur l'Eglise." In *Louis Massignon*, edited by J.-F. Six. Paris: L'Herne, 1970.

Chew, Samuel Claggett. *The Crescent and the Rose*. New York: Oxford University Press, 1937.

Cohn-Sherbok, Dan, ed. *World Religions and Human Liberation*. Maryknoll: N.Y.: Orbis Books, 1992.

Coward, Harold, and Leslie Kawamura, eds. *Religion and Ethnicity*. Waterloo, Ont.: Wilfrid Laurier University Press, 1978.

Cragg, Kenneth. *The Event of the Qur'an*. London: George Allen and Unwin, 1971.

——. *Jesus and the Muslim*. London: George Allen and Unwin, 1985.

——. *The Mind of the Qur'an*. London: George Allen and Unwin, 1973.

——. *Muhammad and the Christian: A Question of Response*. Maryknoll, N.Y.: Orbis Books, 1984.

Crawford, S. Cromwell, ed. *World Religions and Global Ethics*. New York: Paragon House, 1989.

Daghorn, René. *La geste d'Ismael d'après l'onomastique et la tradition arabes*. Geneva: Droz, 1981.

Daniel, Norman. *The Arabs and Medieval Europe*. London: Longman, 1975.

——. *Islam and the West: The Making of an Image*. Edinburgh: Edinburgh University Press, 1960.

Dante (Alighieri). *The Divine Comedy*. Vol. 1: *Hell*. Translated by Dorothy L. Sayers, Harmondsworth, Middlesex: Penguin Books, 1949.

Dawe, Donald G., and John B. Carman, eds. *Christian Faith in a Religiously Plural World*. Maryknoll, N.Y.: Orbis Books, 1978.

Dawson, Christopher. *The Making of Europe*. London: Sheed and Ward, 1932.

Denny, Frederick M., and Rodney L. Taylor, eds. *The Holy Book in Comparative Perspective*. Columbia, S.C.: University of South Carolina Press, 1985.

De Rosa, Peter. *Christ and Original Sin*. Milwaukee, Wis.: Bruce, 1967.

Di Bernardino, Angelo., ed. *Encyclopedia of the Early Church*. New York: Oxford University Press, 1992.

Drummond, R. H. "Towards a Theological Understanding of Islam." *Journal of Ecumenical Studies* 9/4 (1972): 777-801.

Dulles, Avery. *Models of Revelation*. Garden City, N.Y.: Doubleday, 1983.

Dupuis, Jacques. *Jesus Christ at the Encounter of World Religions*. Maryknoll, N.Y.: Orbis Books, 1991.

Duran, Khalid. "Interreligious Dialogue and the Islamic 'Original Sin.'" In *Muslims in Dialogue*, edited by Leonard Swidler. Lewiston, N.Y.: Edwin Mellen Press, 1992.

——. "Muslims and Non-Muslims." In *Muslims in Dialogue,* edited by Leonard Swidler. Lewiston, N.Y.: Edwin Mellen Press, 1992.

Eliade, Mircea, ed. *The Encyclopedia of Religion*. New York: Macmillan, 1987.

Engineer, Asghar Ali. *Islam and Liberation Theology: Essays on Liberative Elements in Islam*. New Delhi: Sterling Publishers, 1990.

Esposito, John L. *Islam: The Straight Path.* New York: Oxford University Press, 1991.

——————. *Islam and Politics.* Syracuse, N.Y.: Syracuse University Press, 1984.

——————. *The Islamic Threat: Myth or Reality?* New York: Oxford University Press, 1992.

Esposito, John L., ed. *The Oxford Encyclopedia of the Modern Islamic World.* New York: Oxford University Press, 1995.

Fiorenza, Francis Schüssler, and John P. Gavin, eds. *Systematic Theology: Roman Catholic Perspectives.* Dublin: Gill and Macmillan, 1992.

Fisher, Sydney Nettleton. *The Middle East: A History.* London: Routledge and Kegan Paul, 1971.

Freemantle, Anne. *Desert Calling: The Life of Charles de Foucauld.* London: Hollis and Carter, 1950.

Gaudeul, Jean-Marie. *Encounters and Clashes: Islam and Christianity in History.* 2 vols. Rome: Pontificio Istituto di Studi Arabi e Islamici, 1990.

Geffré, Claude. "Le Coran, une parole de Dieu différente?" *Lumière et Vie* 32 (1983): 21-32.

Gerholm, Tomas, and Yngve Georg Lithman, eds. *The New Islamic Presence in Europe.* London and New York: Mansell Publishing, 1988.

Gibb, H. A. R. *Mohammedanism.* 2d revised edition. London: Oxford University Press, 1980.

Gibbon, Edward. *The Decline and Fall of the Roman Empire.* New York: The Modern Library, n.d.

Gilkey, Langdon. *Message and Existence.* San Francisco: Harper & Row, 1978.

Gilson, Etienne. *History of Christian Philosophy in the Middle Ages.* New York: Random House, 1955.

Glazier, Michael, and Monica Hellwig, eds. *The Modern Catholic Encyclopedia.* Collegeville, Minn.: The Liturgical Press, 1994.

Goddard, Hugh. *Christians and Muslims: From Double Standards to Mutual Understanding.* Richmond, Surrey: Curzon Press, 1995.

——————. *Islam: Towards a Christian Assessment.* Oxford: Latimer House, 1992.

——————. *Muslim Perspectives of Christianity.* London: Grey Seal, 1996.

Goldschmidt, Arthur, Jr. *A Concise History of the Middle East.* 3d edition. Boulder, Colo.: Westview Press, 1988.

Goldziher, Ignaz. *Introduction to Islamic Theology and Law.* Translated by Andras and Ruth Hamori. Princeton: Princeton University Press, 1981.

Grant, Robert M. *Religion and Politics at the Council of Nicaea.* Chicago: University of Chicago Press, 1973.

Griffith, Sydney H. "The Gospel in Arabic: An Inquiry into Its Appearance in the First Abbasid Century." *Oriens Christianus* 69 (1985): 126-67.

Griffiths, Paul J., ed. *Christianity through Non-Christian Eyes.* Maryknoll, N.Y.: Orbis Books, 1990.

Grose, George B., and Benjamin J. Hubbard, eds. *The Abraham Connection: A Jew, Christian and Muslim in Dialogue.* Notre Dame, Ind.: Cross Cultural Publications, 1994.

Haddad, Yvonne Yazbeck, and Adair T. Lummis. *Islamic Values in the United States.* New York: Oxford University Press, 1987.

Haddad, Yvonne Yazbeck, and Wadi Zaidan Haddad, eds. *Christian-Muslim Encounters*. Gainesville, Fla.: University Press of Florida, 1995.

Haddad, Yvonne Yazbeck, and Jane Idleman Smith, eds. *Muslim Communities in North America*. Albany: State University of New York Press, 1994.

Haines, Byron L., and Frank L. Cooley, eds. *Christians and Muslims Together— An Exploration by Presbyterians*. Philadelphia: The Geneva Press, 1987.

Haskins, Charles H. *The Renaissance of the Twelfth Century*. Cambridge, Mass.: Harvard University Press, 1927.

Hassan, Riffat. "On Human Rights and the Qur'anic Perspective." In *Muslims in Dialogue,* edited by Leonard Swidler. Lewiston, N.Y.: Edwin Mellen Press, 1992.

Hayek, Michel. *Le Mystère d'Ismael*. Paris: Maison Mame, 1964.

Hick, John. *Evil and the God of Love*. San Francisco: Harper & Row, 1978.

Hick, John. "Trinity and Incarnation in the Light of Religious Pluralism." In *Three Faiths—One God,* edited by John Hick and Edmund S. Meltzer. Albany, N.Y.: State University of New York Press, 1989.

Hick, John., ed. *The Myth of God Incarnate*. London: SCM Press, 1977.

Hick, John, and Paul F. Knitter, eds. *The Myth of Christian Uniqueness*. Maryknoll, N.Y.: Orbis Books, 1987.

Hick, John, and Edmund S. Meltzer, eds. *Three Faiths—One God*. Albany, N.Y.: State University of New York Press, 1989.

Hodgson, Marshall, G. S. *The Venture of Islam*. Chicago: University of Chicago Press, 1974.

Hourani, A. H. *Minorities in the Arab World*. London: Oxford University Press, 1947.

Husaini, Zohra. *Muslims in the Canadian Mosaic: Socio-Cultural and Economic Links with Their Countries of Origin*. Edmonton, Alberta: Muslim Research Foundation, 1990.

Husayn, Muhammad Kamil. *City of Wrong*. Translated by Kenneth Cragg. Amsterdam: Djambatan, 1959.

Ibn 'Ata' Allah. *Kitab al-Hikam*. Translated into English by Victor Danner as *The Book of Wisdom*. In Victor Danner and Wheeler Thackson, *The Book of Wisdom* and *Intimate Conversations*. New York: Paulist Press, 1978.

Ignatius Loyola. *Letters of St. Ignatius of Loyola*. Translated by William J. Young. Chicago: Loyola University Press, 1959.

—————. *The Spiritual Exercises of St. Ignatius*. Translated by Louis J. Puhl. Chicago: Loyola University Press, 1951.

Jackh, Ernst. *Background of the Middle East*. Ithaca, N.Y.: Cornell University Press, 1952.

Jansen, G. H. *Militant Islam*. New York: Harper & Row, 1979.

John Paul II, Pope. "Discourse to Catholic Community in Ankara." *Origins* 9/26 (1979): 419-20.

—————. "Message to Young Muslims in Casablanca." Secretariatus pro Non-Christianis. *Bulletin* 20/3 (1985): 249-57.

—————. *Recognize the Spiritual Bonds Which Unite Us: Sixteen Years of Christian-Muslim Dialogue*. Vatican City: Pontifical Council for Interreligious Dialogue, 1994.

—————. *Redemptor Hominis*. Boston: Daughters of St. Paul, 1979.

—————. *Redemptoris Missio.* In *Redemption and Dialogue,* edited by William R. Burrows. Maryknoll, N.Y.: Orbis Books, 1993.

Johnson, William, trans. *The Cloud of Unknowing* and *The Book of Privy Counselling.* New York: Image Books, 1973.

Johnstone, Penelope. "Christians and Muslims in Britain." *Islamochristiana* 7 (1981): 167-99; 12 (1986): 181-90.

—————. "An Islamic Perspective on Dialogue." *Islamochristiana* 13 (1987): 131-71.

Kelly, Marjorie, ed. *Islam: The Religious and Political Life of a World Community.* New York: Praeger, 1984.

Khadduri, Majid. *War and Peace in the Law of Islam.* Baltimore: Johns Hopkins Press, 1955.

Khadduri, M., and H. Liebesney, eds. *Law in the Middle East.* Washington, D.C.: Middle East Institute, 1955.

Khoury, Adel-Théodore. *Les théologiens Byzantines et l'Islam.* Louvain: Nauwelaerts, 1969.

Kimball, Charles. *Striving Together: A Way Forward in Christian-Muslim Relations.* Maryknoll, N.Y.: Orbis Books, 1991.

Kitagawa, Joseph Mitsuo. *The Christian Tradition beyond Its European Captivity.* Philadelphia: Trinity Press International, 1992.

Knitter, Paul F. *Jesus and the Other Names.* Maryknoll, N.Y.: Orbis Books, 1996.

—————. *No Other Name? A Critical Survey of Christian Attitudes toward World Religions.* Maryknoll, N.Y.: Orbis Books, 1985.

—————. *One Earth Many Religions.* Maryknoll, N.Y.: Orbis Books, 1995.

Kritzeck, James. *Peter the Venerable and Islam.* Princeton: Princeton University Press, 1964.

—————. *Sons of Abraham: Jews, Christians, and Moslems.* Baltimore and Dublin: Helicon, 1965.

Küng, Hans. *Christianity and World Religions.* Garden City, N.Y.: Doubleday, 1986.

—————. *Global Responsibility: In Search of a New World Ethic.* New York: Crossroad, 1991.

Küng, Hans, and Jurgen Moltmann, eds. *The Ethics of the World Religions and Human Rights.* London: SCM Press, 1990.

Küng, Hans, and Karl-Josef Kuschel, eds. *A Global Ethic: The Declaration of the Parliament of the World's Religions.* New York: Continuum, 1993.

Kuschel, Karl-Josef. *Abraham: Sign of Hope for Jews, Christians, and Muslims.* New York: Continuum, 1995.

Latourelle, René. *Theology of Revelation.* Staten Island: Alba House, 1987.

Ledit, Charles-J. *Mahomet, Israel et le Christ.* Paris: La Colombe, 1956.

Lelong, Michael. "Mahomet, prophète de l'Islam." *Studia Missionalia* 33 (1984): 251-76.

Levonian, Lootfy. *Studies in the Relationship between Islam and Christianity.* London: George Allen and Unwin, 1940.

Lewis, Bernard. *Islam and the West.* New York and Oxford: Oxford University Press, 1993.

Lewis, Bernard, and Dominique Schnapper, eds. *Muslims in Europe.* London: Pinter Publishers, 1994.

Lewis, Philip. *Islamic Britain: Religion, Politics, and Identity among British Muslims.* London and New York: I. B. Tauris Publishers, 1994.

Lings, Martin. *What Is Sufism?* Berkeley: University of California Press, 1977.

Martinson, Paul Varo, ed. *Islam: An Introduction for Christians.* Minneapolis: Augsburg, 1994.

Mason, Herbert. *Memoir of a Friend: Louis Massignon.* Notre Dame, Ind.: University of Notre Dame Press, 1988.

Massignon, Louis. "Le Signe Marial." *Rythmes du Monde* 3 (1948): 7-16.

McAuliffe, Jane Damnen. *Qur'anic Christians: An Analysis of Classical and Modern Exegesis.* New York: Cambridge University Press, 1991.

McBrien, Richard P. *Catholicism.* New York: HarperCollins, 1994.

——————, ed. *The HarperCollins Encyclopedia of Catholicism.* New York: HarperCollins, 1995.

McCloud, Aminah Beverly. *African American Islam.* New York and London: Routledge, 1995.

Michel, Thomas. "Christian-Muslim Dialogue in a Changing World." *Theology Digest* 39/4 (1992): 303-20.

——————. "Islamo-Christian Dialogue: Reflections on the Recent Teachings of the Church." Secretariatus pro Non-Christianis. *Bulletin* 20/2 (1985): 172-93.

Míguez Bonino, José. "The Concern for a Vital and Coherent Theology." *Ecumenical Review* 41/2 (1989): 160-76.

Mingana, Alphonse. "The Apology of Timothy the Patriarch before the Caliph Madhi." *Bulletin of the John Rylands Library* 12 (1928): 137-298.

Monro, D. C. "The Speech of Urban II at Clermont, 1095." *American Historical Review* 11 (1905): 231-42.

Moran, Gabriel. *The Present Revelation.* New York: Herder and Herder, 1972.

——————. *Theology of Revelation.* New York: Herder and Herder, 1966.

Moubarac, Youakim. *Abraham dans le Coran.* Paris: J. Vrin, 1958.

Myers, Eugene A. *Arabic Thought and the Western World in the Golden Age of Islam.* New York: Frederick Ungar, 1964.

Nasr, Seyyed Hussein. *Ideals and Realities of Islam.* Boston: Beacon Press, 1966.

——————. *Islamic Spirituality: Foundations.* New York: Crossroad, 1987.

——————. *Islamic Spirituality: Manifestations.* New York: Crossroad, 1991.

Neill, Stephen. *A History of Christian Missions.* Harmondsworth, Middlesex: Penguin Books, 1977.

Nicholson, Reynold A. *The Mystics of Islam.* London: Routledge and Kegan Paul, 1975.

Nielsen, Jorgen. "Great Britain." In *The Oxford Encyclopedia of the Modern Islamic World,* edited by John L. Esposito. Vol. 2. New York: Oxford University Press, 1995.

——————. *Muslims in Western Europe.* Edinburgh: University of Edinburgh Press, 1992.

O'Leary, De Lacy. *Arabic Thought and Its Place in History.* London: Routledge and Kegan Paul, 1963.

——————. *How Greek Science Passed to the Arabs.* London: Routledge and Kegan Paul, 1948.

Parrinder, Geoffrey. *Jesus in the Qur'an.* London: Faber and Faber, 1965.

Paul VI, Pope. *Evangelii Nuntiandi.* London: Catholic Truth Society, 1976.

—————. *Ecclesiam Suam. The Pope Speaks* 10 (1965): 253-92.

Pickthall, Muhammad. *The Meaning of the Glorious Koran.* New York: New American Library, 1953.

Rahman, Fazlur. *Major Themes of the Qur'an.* Chicago: Bibliotheca Islamica, 1980.

Rahner, Karl. "Christianity and Non-Christian Religions." *Theological Investigations.* Vol. 5. London: Darton, Longman, and Todd, 1966; Baltimore: Helicon Press, 1966.

—————. *The Dynamic Element in the Church.* Montreal: Palm Publishers, 1964.

—————. *Foundations of Christian Faith.* New York: Seabury Press, 1978.

—————. "History of the World and Salvation History." *Theological Investigations.* Vol. 5. London: Darton, Longman, and Todd, 1966.

—————. "Remarks on the Dogmatic Treatise *'De Trinitate.'*" *Theological Investigations.* Vol. 4. Baltimore: Helicon Press, 1966.

—————. "Toward a Fundamental Theological Interpretation of Vatican II," *Theological Studies* 40/4 (1979): 716-27.

Raiser, Konrad. *Ecumenism in Transition: A Paradigm Shift in the Ecumenical Movement?* Geneva: World Council of Churches, 1991.

Richardson, Alan. *Creeds in the Making.* London: SCM Press, 1961.

Robinson, Neal. "Massignon, Vatican II, and Islam as an Abrahamic Religion." *Islam and Christian-Muslim Relations* 2/2 (1991): 182-205.

Rockfeller, Steven C., and John C. Elder, eds. *Spirit and Nature: Why the Environment Is a Religious Issue.* Boston: Beacon Press, 1992.

Rodinson, Maxime. *Europe and the Mystique of Islam.* Seattle: University of Washington Press, 1987.

Rondet, Henri. *Original Sin: The Patristic and Theological Background.* Shannon, Ireland: Ecclesia Press, 1972.

Rosenthal, E. I. J. *Political Thought in Medieval Islam.* Cambridge: Cambridge University Press, 1968.

Rouner, Leroy S., ed. *Human Rights and the World's Religions.* Notre Dame, Ind.: University of Notre Dame Press, 1988.

Rousseau, Richard W., ed. *Christianity and Islam: The Struggling Dialogue.* Montrose, Pa.: Ridge Row Press, 1985.

Sahas, Daniel J. *John of Damascus on Islam.* Leiden: E. J. Brill, 1972.

Samartha, Stanley. *Courage for Dialogue: Ecumenical Issues in Interreligious Relationships.* Geneva: World Council of Churches, 1981.

Sarton, George. *Introduction to the History of Science.* Vol. 1. Baltimore: Williams and Wilkins, 1927.

Schacht, J., and C. E. Bosworth, eds. *The Legacy of Islam.* Oxford: Oxford University Press, 1979.

Schimmel, Annemarie. *Mystical Dimensions of Islam.* Chapel Hill, N.C.: University of North Carolina Press, 1975.

Schoonenberg, Piet. *Man and Sin.* London: Sheed and Ward, 1965.

Shadid, W. A. R., and P. S. Koningsveld, eds. *The Integration of Islam and Hinduism in Western Europe.* Kampen, The Netherlands: Kok Pharos Publishing House, 1991.

Sherif, Faruq. *A Guide to the Contents of the Qur'an*. Reading, UK: Ithaca Press, 1995.

Shorter, Aylward. *Revelation and Its Interpretation*. London: G. Chapman, 1983.

Siddiqi, Muzammil H. "A Muslim Response to John Hick: Trinity and Incarnation in the Light of Religious Pluralism." In *Three Faiths—One God*, edited by John Hick and Edmund S. Meltzer. Albany, N.Y.: State University of New York Press, 1989.

Smith, Byron Porter. *Islam in English Literature*. Edited with an introduction by S. B. Bushrui and Anahid Melikian and a foreword by Omar A. Farrukh. Delmar, N.Y.: Caravan Books, 1977.

Smith, Margaret. *Studies in Early Mysticism in the Near and Middle East*. London: Sheldon Press, 1931.

Smith, Wilfred Cantwell. *Islam in Modern History*. Princeton: Princeton University Press, 1957.

Southern, Richard William. *Western Views of Islam in the Middle Ages*. Cambridge, Mass.: Harvard University Press, 1962.

Speelman, Gé, Jan van Lin, and Dick Mulder, eds. *Muslims and Christians in Europe Breaking New Ground*. Kampen, The Netherlands: Uitgeverij Kok, 1993.

Speight, R. Marston. "Christian-Muslim Dialogue in the United States of America." *Islamochristiana* 7 (1981): 201-10.

—————. *Christian-Muslim Relations: An Introduction for Christians in the United States of America*. Hartford, Conn.: Task Force on Christian-Muslim Relations, National Council of the Churches of Christ in the USA, 1983.

Stoddart, William. *Sufism*. Wellingborough, UK: The Aquarian Press, 1982.

Swidler, Leonard. *The Meaning of Life at the Edge of the Third Millennium*. New York: Paulist Press, 1992.

—————, ed. *Muslims in Dialogue*. Lewiston, N.Y.: Edwin Mellen Press, 1992.

—————, ed. *Religious Liberty and Human Rights in Nations and in Religions*. Philadelphia: Ecumenical Press, 1986.

—————, ed. *Toward a Universal Theology of Religion*. Maryknoll, N.Y.: Orbis Books, 1988.

Talbi, Mohamed. "Islam and Dialogue—Some Reflections on a Current Topic." In *Christianity and Islam: The Struggling Dialogue*, edited by Richard W. Rousseau. Montrose, Pa.: Ridge Row Press, 1985. The essay also appears in *Christianity through Non-Christian Eyes*, ed. Paul J. Griffiths. Maryknoll, N.Y.: Orbis Books, 1990.

—————. "Possibilities and Conditions for a Better Understanding between Islam and the West." In *Muslims in Dialogue*, edited by Leonard Swidler. Lewiston, N.Y.: Edwin Mellen Press, 1992.

Tennant, F. R. *The Sources of the Doctrines of the Fall and Original Sin*. New York: Schocken Books, 1968.

Tritton, A. S. *The Caliphs and Their Non-Christian Subjects: A Critical Study of the Covenant of 'Umar*. London: Oxford University Press, 1930.

"Universal Declaration on Human Rights in Islam." *Islamochristiana* 9 (1983): 103-20.

Vander Werff, Lyle L. *Christian Mission to Muslims*. South Pasadena: W. Carey Library, 1977.

Vaporis, N. M., ed. *Orthodox Christians and Muslims.* Brookline, Mass.: Holy Cross Orthodox Press, 1986.

Vertin, Michael., ed. *Appropriating the Lonergan Idea.* Washington, D.C.: The Catholic University of America Press, 1989.

Von Grunebaum, Gustave E. *Medieval Islam: A Study in Cultural Orientation.* Chicago: University of Chicago Press, 1946.

Walzer, Richard. *Greek into Arabic: Essays on Islamic Philosophy.* Oxford: Bruno Cassirer, 1962.

Watt, W. Montgomery. *Bell's Introduction to the Qur'an.* Edinburgh: Edinburgh University Press, 1970.

―――――. *The Influence of Islam on Medieval Europe.* Edinburgh: Edinburgh University Press, 1972.

―――――. *Islam and Christianity Today.* London: Routledge and Kegan Paul, 1983.

―――――. *Islamic Revelation in the Modern World.* Edinburgh: Edinburgh University Press, 1969.

―――――. *Muhammad: Prophet and Statesman.* London: Oxford University Press, 1961.

―――――. *Muslim-Christian Encounters.* London and New York: Routledge, 1991.

Waugh, Earle H., Sharon McIrvin Abu Laban, and Regula Burckhardt Qureshi, eds. *Muslim Families in North America.* Edmonton, Alberta: The University of Alberta Press, 1991.

Women's Committee of the Muslim Students Association. *Parents' Manual: A Guide for Muslim Parents Living in North America.* Brentwood, Md.: American Trust Publications, 1976.

World Council of Churches. *Christians Meeting Muslims: WCC Papers on Ten Years of Christian-Muslim Dialogue.* Geneva: World Council of Churches, 1977.

―――――. *Christian-Muslim Dialogue: Papers Presented at the Broumana Consultation, 12-18 July 1972.* Edited by S. J. Samartha and J. B. Taylor. Geneva: World Council of Churches, 1973.

―――――. *Guidelines on Dialogue with People of Living Faiths and Ideologies.* Geneva: World Council of Churches, 1979.

―――――. *Meeting in Faith: Twenty Years of Christian-Muslim Conversations Sponsored by the World Council of Churches.* Compiled by Stuart E. Brown. Geneva: World Council of Churches, 1989.

Zaehner, R. C. *At Sundry Times: An Essay in the Comparison of Religions.* London: Faber and Faber, 1958.

Zebiri, Kate. *Muslims and Christians Face to Face.* Oxford: Oneworld, 1997.

Glossary

aman	permission granted to a non-Muslim to live in territory under Muslim rule for a period of less than a year.
asbab al-nuzul	occasions of revelation.
aya (ayat)	verse (verses) of the Qur'an.
Ashura	the tenth day of Muharram, the first month of the Muslim calendar.
ayatollah	the title of highest rank among religious leaders in Twelver Shi'ism.
badaliyya movement	a sodality founded by Louis Massignon, in 1934, whose members believe that Christians and Muslims form a community of faith. This belief is based on a doctrine that the Holy Spirit is at work in Islam as well as in Christianity.
caliph	in Sunni Islam, a successor to the Prophet Muhammad who was designated by the community to head the Muslim state.
dar al-Islam	territories governed by Islamic law.
dar al-harb	territories not governed by Islamic law.
darura	the principle of necessity in Islamic law.
darvish	a member of any Islamic religious order; a faqir; a dervish.
daw'ah	a religious outreach or mission to exhort people to embrace Islam.
dhikr	the Islamic rite of repeating the name of God or a Qur'anic phrase, either vocally or silently, so as to become aware of God.
dhimmi	tolerated People of the Book (primarily Jews and Christians) living within lands under Muslim rule with the right of retaining their non-Muslim status

	in exchange for payment of a poll tax and observing other obligations to the Muslim body politic.
fana	in Sufism, the disappearance of the ego or total self-forgetfulness.
faqir	a member of any Islamic religious order; a dervish. *Al-fuqara*, the plural form, means "the poor."
Fatiha	the opening chapter of the Qur'an.
hadith	a narrative report of what Muhammad said or did.
hajj	pilgrimage to Mecca, the fifth pillar of Islam.
hijra	the migration of Muhammad and his followers from Mecca to Yathrib/Medina in 622; the beginning of the Muslim era.
ijma	the consensus of the community.
'ilm	a technical term for intellectual knowledge as opposed to experiential knowledge.
Imam	in Shi'ism the name for the specially revered descendants of Ali, Muhammad's cousin, who ruled the Shi'i community during the early centuries.
jihad	striving in the cause of God. This striving is divided into two categories. The great jihad is the warfare in oneself against any evil or temptation. The lesser jihad is the defense of Islam, or of a Muslim country or community, against aggression. Jihad as "holy war" must be understood in this context.
jizya	the per capita tax paid by People of the Book (primarily Jews and Christians).
Ka'ba	the cube-shaped stone building in the center of the Great Mosque in Mecca founded, according to Islamic tradition, by Abraham and Ishmael.
ma'rifat	in Sufism, direct knowledge of God as opposed to intellectual knowledge.
marja' al-taqlid	the living representative of the Hidden Imam in Twelver Shi'ism.
Muharram	the first month of the Muslim calendar.
mullah	the title of lowest rank among religious leaders in Twelver Shi'ism.

musta'min	a temporary resident in territory under Muslim rule.
qiyas	analogy.
Ramadan	the ninth month of the Muslim calendar, during which Muslims have a duty to fast.
salat	ritual prayer, the second pillar of Islam.
sawn	fasting, the fourth pillar of Islam.
shahada	the profession of faith that "there is no god but God, and Muhammad is the Prophet of God"; the first pillar of Islam.
shari'a	the religious law of Islam, which is derived from revelation (Qur'an) and the example of Muhammad (*sunna, hadith*).
Shi'ite	a name for a minority of Muslims who trace their spiritual heritage to Muhammad through his cousin Ali.
shaykh	the leader of a Sufi order.
Sufi	an Islamic ascetic or mystic who belongs to a religious order.
sunna	the record of what Muhammad said and did.
Sunnis	a designation of the vast majority of Muslims who do not acknowledge the authority of Shi'i Imams.
sura	a chapter of the Qur'an.
tariqa	a community of Sufi mystics.
ulema	religious teachers of Islam responsible for interpreting the divine law and administrating the community's affairs.
ummi	unlettered, illiterate.
wahy	the special revelation that God gives to prophets.
zakat	almsgiving, the third pillar of Islam.

Index

Other Titles in the Faith Meets Faith Series

P6Z